DE CHIRICO: *The Disquieting Muses.*

Twentieth-Century **Italian** Art

BY JAMES THRALL SOBY

AND ALFRED H. BARR, JR.

The Museum of Modern Art

New York

Contents

	PAGE
Honorary Committee	4
Foreword	5
Acknowledgments	6
Early Futurism BY A. H. B., JR.	7
The *Scuola Metafisica* BY J. T. S.	17
Amedeo Modigliani BY J. T. S.	24
Painting and Sculpture since 1920 BY J. T. S.	25
Later Work of de Chirico, Carrà and Morandi	25
The *Novecento*	26
The Middle Generation	28
Two Realists: Rosai and Donghi	29
The Roman School	30
The Fantasts	31
The Younger Abstractionists; the *Fronte nuovo delle arti*	31
Recent Sculpture	33
Color Plates	
De Chirico: *The Disquieting Muses*	frontispiece
Boccioni: *States of Mind, I: The Farewells*	opp. p. 8
Modigliani: *Woman with a Necklace*	opp. p. 24
Morandi: *Still Life*	opp. p. 26
Guttuso: *The Maffia*	opp. p. 32
Plates	35
Catalog of the Exhibition	125
Bibliography BY BERNARD KARPEL	136

Executive Secretary
for the Exhibition in Italy:
Romeo Toninelli, Milan

Honorary Committee

Prof. Giulio Carlo Argan, Rome

Dr. Palma Bucarelli, Rome

Carlo Cardazzo, Venice

Raffaele Carrieri, Milan

Dr. Pietro Feroldi, Brescia

Dr. Riccardo Gualino, Rome

Riccardo Jucker, Milan

Prof. Roberto Longhi, Florence

Donna Benedetta Marinetti, Rome

Viscount Dr. Franco Marmont, Milan

Dr. Gianni Mattioli, Milan

Adriano Pallini, Milan

Prof. Rodolfo Pallucchini, Venice

Dr. Camillo Poli, Milan

Dr. Pietro Rollino, Rome

Giovanni Scheiwiller, Milan

Cesare Tosi, Milan

Dr. Lionello Venturi, Rome

Dr. Mario F. Vespa, Genoa

4

Foreword

This book and the exhibition on which it is based have been planned as a general introduction to modern Italian art. The field is one that we in America have tended to neglect, not only because of our rightful interest in our own contemporary painting and sculpture, but also because of two formidable counter-attractions in Europe—the Parisian present and the Italian past.

But twentieth-century Italian art is well worth our attention. It has produced two movements—Futurism and the *scuola metafisica*—which have made vital contributions to the international mainstream of art in our time. These two movements have been examined in some detail in the following pages. With more recent Italian developments our method has been less methodical. We have illustrated a wide but by no means comprehensive selection of art produced by leaders of the older and middle generations, men who have not been associated with the two movements just mentioned or who in later years have turned away from them. We have also included a group of artists who have attained national and occasionally international prominence chiefly during and since the recent war. There have been cases in which we have not been able to borrow abroad works which we had hoped to exhibit.

The climate for art is propitious in Italy just now, with the shackles of Fascist isolationism rusting empty on the ground, and we have sought—again without claim to finality—to indicate what directions the newer creative impetus is taking.

J.T.S.

A.H.B., JR.

Acknowledgments

On behalf of the Trustees of the Museum of Modern Art we wish to express our gratitude to The Honorable James C. Dunn, United States Ambassador to Italy, and to Mrs. Dunn, for their sympathetic interest in the exhibition and for their kindness to staff members while the latter were in Rome. We are equally indebted to His Excellency Alberto Tarchiani, Italian Ambassador to the United States, and to the Marchese Taliani de Marchio, Chief of Protocol of the Italian Foreign Office, who have graciously expressed their appreciation of the exhibition as a means toward closer cultural relations between our two nations.

Without the initiative, efficient services and generous support of the exhibition's Executive Secretary in Italy, Romeo Toninelli, the exhibition would not have been possible. We are greatly indebted to him, and should like to extend our thanks for his major part in the exhibition.

We also wish to thank Dr. Fernanda Wittgens, Supervisor of the Art Galleries of Lombardy, and Prof. Costantino Baroni, Director of the Civic Museums of Milan, for placing at our disposal the facilities of the Castello Sforzesco as a point of assembly for the works borrowed in Italy.

The Compagnia Italiana di Navigazione Fratelli Cosulich of Genoa and the Gdynia-American Line of New York have generously arranged special transportation for most of the works in the exhibition, and we are grateful to them.

Mr. Laurance P. Roberts, Director of the American Academy at Rome, and Mrs. Roberts, have been extremely helpful during the long course of the exhibition's preparation, and were the gracious hosts of its directors and their wives during their stay in Rome. Miss Isabella Panzini, then of the Academy's staff, aided greatly with details of the exhibition.

We should also like to record our appreciation of invaluable help from the following:

Milan: Countess Elena Amor de Celani, Raffaele Carrieri, Carlo Frua de Angeli, Prof. Virginio Ghiringelli and Lamberto Vitali.

Rome: Princess Margherita Caetani di Bassiano; Mr. and Mrs. Paul Hyde Bonner; Dr. Palma Bucarelli, Supervisor of the National Gallery of Modern Art; Princess Laetitia Boncompagni di Venosa; Donna Benedetta Marinetti; Prof. and Mrs. C. Rufus Morey; Dr. Lionello Venturi.

Venice: Dr. Umbro Apollonio of the Biennial Exposition; Mr. and Mrs. Vieri Freccia; Prof. Rodolfo Pallucchini, Secretary-General of the Biennial Exposition.

Dr. Max Ascoli and Vico Baer of New York, and Douglas Cooper of London have given us valuable counsel, for which we extend our thanks.

We wish to acknowledge the active help of our wives in the exhibition's preparation and to mention special aid from Monroe Wheeler, Director of Exhibitions and Publications; his assistant, Miss Frances Keech; Miss Dorothy Dudley, Registrar; Miss Alice Bacon of the Department of Painting and Sculpture; and Miss Francis Pernas, Miss Ellin Roudin and Edward Mills of the Publications Department.

JAMES THRALL SOBY
ALFRED H. BARR, JR.
Directors of the Exhibition

Early Futurism

In the year 1909, dreaming of her past, Italy slumbered—or so it seemed to certain young Milanese. In politics, Premier Giolitti was ingeniously balancing Parliament, labor, business, the Church; compromising, conciliating, effecting a certain material prosperity in spite of social unrest; weaving an intricate path between reaction on the right, anarchism and syndicalism on the left. In philosophy, the Neapolitan school flourished under Croce and Gentile, systematic, scholarly, history-minded. In literature honors were divided between Pascoli, a sensitive lyric poet, traditional in spirit and like his master, the pessimistic Carducci, a professor at the University of Bologna; and d'Annunzio, erotic melodramatist, celebrant of Italy's Middle Ages and Renaissance and, above all, of Venice. In music the vacillating Boito lingered for the forty-seventh year over his opera *Nero*; Puccini, five years after *Madame Butterfly*, was at work on *La Fanciulla del West*; and Busoni was in Berlin emulating Liszt by re-arranging Bach. Italian films led the world but they were "epics" of Antiquity which were to culminate shortly in *Quo Vadis*, *The Last Days of Pompeii* and finally, *Cabiria*, a superfilm of the Punic Wars. Among painters of reputation Mancini held the field in Rome, recalling late Titian and Rembrandt with rich virtuosity; Boldini in Paris was out-Sargenting Sargent; Sartorio admired d'Annunzio and painted like Böcklin; the languid "pittori lirici" looked back to the English Pre-Raphaelites; and the last of the *Macchiaioli* remembered Fattori and other Italian equivalents of Manet or Winslow Homer. The successful sculptors were clever modelers like the aging Gemito who had flourished since his *Fisherboy* had been bought by Meissonier; but Medardo Rosso, revolutionary precursor of Rodin at his boldest, was officially neglected. Neglected, too, were the most modern painters of the period, the divisionists, who worked in a style parallel to French neo-impressionism of the 1890's. Their leader, Segantini, had been dead ten years.

Yet in this easy-going, unambitious, retrospective, peninsular Italy of 1909, there were already rumblings and cracklings of an aggressive modernism. The year before, in Florence, Prezzolini had founded the periodical *La Voce* which published brilliant, modern, internationally-minded criticism by Giovanni Papini and Ardengo Soffici, the latter a young painter just back from Paris. And in Milan, Filippo Tommaso Marinetti, wealthy, educated at the Sorbonne, a poet and dramatist, a declaimer of French and Italian poetry, the founder and editor of *Poesia*, was preparing an explosion. On the 20th of February, 1909, his play, *Le Roi Bombance*, a burlesque à la Jarry, opened in Paris at the Théâtre de l'Oeuvre. On the same day, Marinetti published in *Figaro*, the Paris newspaper for which he was the Italian literary correspondent, the first

Manifesto of Futurism

We shall sing the love of danger, energy and boldness. . . .

We declare that the world's splendor has been enriched by a new beauty: the beauty of speed. A racing motor-car, its hood adorned with great pipes like snakes with explosive breath . . . a roaring motor-car, which runs like a machine gun, is more beautiful than the *Winged Victory of Samothrace*.

We stand upon the topmost crest of the centuries! . . . Why should we look behind us, when we have to smash in the mysterious portals of the Impossible? . . .

We wish to glorify War—the only health giver of the world—militarism, patriotism, the destructive arm of the Anarchist, the beautiful Ideas that kill, the contempt for women. . . .

We wish to destroy the museums, the libraries, to fight against moralism, feminism and all opportunistic and utilitarian meannesses. . . .

It is in Italy that we launch this manifesto of violence, destructive and incendiary, by which we this day found Futurism, because we would deliver Italy from its plague of professors, archaeologists, tourist guides and antique dealers. . . .

The oldest amongst us is thirty; we have, therefore, ten years at least to accomplish our task. When we are forty,

7

let others, younger and more valiant, throw us into the wastebasket like useless manuscripts!

We stand upon the summit of the world and once more we cast our challenge to the stars!

Marinetti's call to arms aroused considerable interest in Paris and, as he had hoped, it electrified the youthful Milanese. The band of Futurist writers grew and was soon joined by three young painters, Boccioni, Carrà and Russolo. They had known each other for over a year and were already united in revolt against the stale air of artistic Milan where the Lombard divisionists were still considered too radical for academic tolerance. Carlo Carrà, born in 1881, had worked with the two best painters in Milan, the realist Tallone and the poetic Previati. Umberto Boccioni, born in Calabria in 1882, had studied with the most advanced painter in Rome, the divisionist Giacomo Balla. In 1904, with his master Balla and his fellow student Gino Severini, Boccioni had helped organize the first Roman *salon des refusés*. In 1907, he settled in Milan and in January, 1909, conspired with Carrà and Luigi Russolo to put on a rebel section in the staid annual exhibition of the society *Famiglia artistica*.

About a year later, after discussions with Marinetti, Boccioni, Carrà and Russolo began work on their own manifesto. Boccioni wrote his friends Balla in Rome and Severini in Paris and got them to join with the Milanese trio in signing their proclamation, dated February 11, 1910:

Manifesto of the Futurist Painters

To the young artists of Italy!

By associating our ideals with those of the futurist poets we are launching a cry of rebellion. . . .

We want rabidly to fight the fanatical, lifeless and snobbish cult of the past which is fed by the deplorable existence of museums. . . .

For other countries Italy still seems the land of the dead, a huge Pompeii white with graves. But actually Italy is coming alive and her political rebirth is now followed by her intellectual rebirth. In the country of illiterates schools multiply; in the country of *dolce far niente* countless factories roar; in the country of traditional esthetics inspirations sparkling with novelty are taking flight today. . . .

Art is vital only when it is grounded in its environment. Our ancestors drew their artistic material from the religious atmosphere that weighed upon their souls and in the same way we must draw our inspiration from the tangible miracles of contemporary life, from the iron net of speed that envelops the earth, from ocean liners, from dreadnoughts, from marvelous flights that plough the skies, from the dark daring of underwater navigators, from the anguished struggle in the conquest of the unknown. And can we remain insensitive to the frenzied activities of great capital cities, to the new psychology of night life, to the hectic figures of the *viveur*, the *cocotte*, the *apache* and the intoxicated? . . .

We propose:

. . . To exalt every form of originality even if reckless, even if over-violent. . . .

To consider art critics useless and harmful. . . .

To rebel against the tyranny of the words "harmony" and "good taste," expressions so elastic that with them one might easily demolish the work of Rembrandt, Goya and Rodin. . . .

To render and glorify the life of today, incessantly and tumultuously transformed by the victories of science. . . .

A month later, March 8, 1910, at the big Chiarella theatre in Turin, the three Milanese painters took part with Marinetti in their first "Futurist Evening." Boccioni read their new Manifesto to an outraged public which had already hissed verses from Dante's *Divine Comedy* under the mistaken impression that they too were Futurist poetry. Carrà then denounced the Italian critics "who didn't know the difference between Cézanne and Ettore Tito" and the evening ended in a riot. Other evenings followed in Milan and other cities. At Bologna, Carrà was nearly struck by the back of a bench hurled from a balcony. In Treviso the Futurists were rescued from a furious citizenry by the police. Marinetti bearded the Austrians in Trieste, and, with the three painters, assaulted d'Annunzio's Venice in the manifesto *Contro Venezia Passatista*. (D'Annunzio countered by making the hero of his new novel an airplane pilot.)

A month after the Turin riot, the five artists signed an explanatory statement, dated April 11:

Technical Manifesto of Futurist Painting

. . . Our thirst for truth can no longer be assuaged by traditional form and color!

A gesture for us will no longer be an *arrested moment* within the universal dynamism: it will be, definitely, *dynamic sensation* itself. . . .

BOCCIONI: *States of Mind, I: The Farewells*, 1911. Oil on canvas, 27⅞ x 37⅞″. Collection Donna Benedetta Marinetti, Rome.

Everything is moving, everything is running, everything is whirling. A figure never stands passively before us, but appears and disappears constantly. Thanks to the persistence of images on the retina, forms in movement are multiplied, deformed, follow one another like vibrations in the space through which they pass. Thus a running horse does not have four legs: he has twenty and their movements are triangular. . . .

The sixteen people around you in a moving tram are one, ten, four, three: they are still and they move; they come and go, they rattle along the street, they are devoured by a patch of sunlight, they sit down again—persistent symbols of universal vibration. And sometimes on the cheek of the person we are speaking to on the street we see a horse passing by at a distance. Our bodies penetrate the couches on which we sit, the couches penetrate us, just as the tram going by enters the houses which, in their turn, fall upon the tram and become amalgamated with it.

. . . Painters have always shown us figures and objects arranged in front of us. We are going to put the spectator at the center of the picture.

We proclaim . . . that universal dynamism must be rendered as dynamic sensation; that movement and light destroy the substance of objects.

We are fighting . . . against the superficial and elementary archaism based on flat tints which reduces painting to an impotent synthesis, infantile and grotesque; against the nude in painting which has become as boring and nauseating as adultery in literature.

We are the primitives of a new and completely transformed sensibility.

After reading these manifestoes so full of youthful bombast, Bergsonian metaphysics, reckless iconoclasm and defiant patriotism, the early paintings of the Milanese Futurists—at least what is left of them—seem an anticlimax. Almost all the Carràs and Russolos of 1910 have, in fact, disappeared. There are a few Boccionis of Milanese industrial suburbs or small excited crowd scenes painted in a meticulous, neo-impressionist, or divisionist dot technique. And there is *The City Rises*, Boccioni's panorama of building construction, the energies of modern technology symbolized not by machines as one might expect from the Futurist manifestoes, but by two colossal horses and their drivers straining at their work. The large drawing (pl. 2) gives some idea of how the forms in this painting seem fused in a kind of flowing radiance, as if painted with an electric brush.

The *Street Pavers* (pl. 1), somewhat later in style, combines divisionist breaking up of light into color spots with cubist breaking up of form into angular planes.

After more demonstrations which included a riotous evening in Rome, the trio held their second show in Milan at the Ricordi Pavilion in the early summer of 1911. A list of the exhibition is not available, but the show probably included two large works by Boccioni, *The City Rises* and *The Laugh*, a garish night-life scene in which the round gaping face of a belly-laughing woman seems to shatter tables, shirt fronts, glasses and bright gowns into a fantasmagoria of color sliced by light rays. Boccioni's chief new work comprised three canvases illustrating *States of Mind*. The large preliminary drawings (pls. 3-5) reveal a rather obvious and naïve use of abstract lines for symbolic and emotional effects. In *The Farewells*, whirling, twisting lines amplify the figures and gestures of the leave-takers. In *Those Who Go*, sharp blade-shaped lines streak across the surface veiling half-seen fragments of the faces of the travelers, while telegraph poles, trees and houses flicker by, merging with the inside of the train along the lines of the paragraph in the *Technical Manifesto* which describes the interior-exterior of a tram in motion. In the third drawing, the figures of those left behind walk slowly away from the station through curtains of drooping, dejected lines.

The canvases themselves were repainted after a trip to Paris in the fall (pls. 6, 7 and color plate opposite page 8). By comparison with the drawings, the paintings in their revised version are more developed and less obvious. They well demonstrate the Futurist effort to present simultaneously subjective feeling and the complex sensations of movement or flux.

Carrà's large Futurist painting, the *Funeral of the Anarchist Galli*, was also finished in 1911 (pl. 18). In his autobiography he describes how, in 1904, he was watching the funeral of the assassinated radical on its way to the Musocco Cemetery. A riot broke out against the squadron of mounted police protecting the procession.

"Without wishing to, I found myself in the center of the struggle. I saw the bier covered with the red flag careening on the shoulders of the pallbearers. I saw the horses rear skittishly, canes and lances clashing, so that it seemed to me that the coffin would fall at any moment and be trampled by the horses." It was this experience which led him, six years later, to contribute to the *Technical Manifesto* the phrase, "we are going to put the spectator at the center of the picture"—though Boccioni also claims credit for this idea. The Futurist use of broken silhouettes, interpenetrating lights and shades and the flickering fan-shaped patterns of flailing weapons contributes to the frenzied kinesthesia of the painting. Yet, fundamentally, in its main lines and masses Carrà's *Funeral* is as classically organized as a fifteenth-century battle piece by Paolo Uccello.

Somewhat later in 1911 Carrà painted *The Tram* (pl. 19), which he originally called, *What the Tram Said to Me*. Again the sense of the simultaneity of movement and the sensation of inner and outer space are fused by the fragmentation of forms, lines and color surfaces.

The exhibition at the Ricordi Pavilion produced some blunt criticism by Soffici in *La Voce*. The Florentine, with seven years of Paris behind him, said the Futurists grossly exaggerated their own importance and called their paintings half-baked in comparison with the work of contemporary French masters whose work he accused them of garbling. The Futurists — Marinetti, Boccioni, Russolo and Carrà—took the next train to Florence and found Soffici, Papini and the rest of *La Voce* at the Café Giubbe Rosse. Boccioni hit Soffici and started a fight. They were all taken to the police station, but were released only to renew the brawl in the station the next morning as the Futurists boarded the train back to Milan.

Soffici's criticisms were confirmed by Severini who came down from Paris a few months later. Though he had signed the 1910 manifestoes at Boccioni's persuasion, he found the paintings of the Futurists pretentious, literary and uncertain in style. He insisted that they must come to Paris to make themselves *au courant* with modernism at its source. Together they persuaded Marinetti to pay for the trip, and later in the fall they all arrived in Paris for a reconnaissance. In Severini's company they saw cubist pictures and their painters first hand. At the same time they made arrangements with Félix Fénéon, the manager of the important Bernheim Jeune Gallery, for a great exhibition to be held early in the new year. When they returned to Milan they painted furiously to prepare for the crucial test.

The exhibition opened February 5, 1912 with a stormy oration by Marinetti before a large gathering of the Paris *avant-garde*, many of whom had previously read the various Futurist manifestoes. The French were aware that the Futurists were mounting a frontal assault on French hegemony in the arts; and they were offended by the aggressive belligerence of the Italians. Apollinaire and Salmon took the Futurists fairly seriously, but other critics were condescending or hostile. Modigliani was outraged; Picasso, contemptuous. Yet the general uproar gave the Milanese a sense of success. Carrà's *Funeral of the Anarchist Galli* was reproduced on the front page of *Le Journal* and the publicity was considerable. Severini, however, was embarrassed by what seemed to him provincial chauvinism on the part of his friends, but he found their paintings better integrated in style than those he had criticized in Milan.

Besides the *Funeral*, Carrà showed *The Jolting of a Cab, What the Tram Said to Me, The Milan Station* and several paintings which seemed more static and cubist than Futurist. Boccioni showed the repainted *States of Mind, The Street Enters the House, The City Rises, Forces of the Street,* and *Simultaneous Vision*. Russolo exhibited *A Tram in Motion,* and his most famous work, *The Revolt* (ill. p. 133). The largest painting in the show was the *Pan-Pan at the Monaco* by Severini himself, who for the first time was showing with his fellow Futurists. He had been working for two years on this kaleidoscopic panorama of a night club, using flat, angular fragments of color. He also showed *Recollections of the Voyage,* a composite picture of

Russolo, Carrà, Marinetti, Boccioni and Severini in Paris at the time of the Futurist Exhibition, February, 1912.

trains, trams and buildings, and the *Boulevard*, which well illustrates his early Futurist style (pl. 20).

Although the Paris exhibition was not received with critical enthusiasm, it aroused popular curiosity throughout Europe. From Paris it went to London, accompanied by Boccioni and Marinetti. On the 10th of March, an hour before the press review of the London show, Boccioni wrote to his friend Vico Baer in Milan: "The Paris show has proved to all Europe the existence of a new movement animated by a formidable enthusiasm. . . . My preface to the catalog aroused so much interest that 17,000 copies were printed. The English catalog is fine too. They have added explanations of every painting . . . . which will be useful to these *bestie di Inglesi*—these stupid Englishmen—as Benvenuto Cellini used to call them. Anyway, the public is imbecile in all countries, and just as it does not understand in Italy, it does not understand here, and it does not understand in France.

"Those here abroad who know Italy and the infantile, ignoble, vulgar condition of its esthetic standards, cannot understand how we have been able to escape from the mud puddle, and thereby, with one leap, put Italian art side by side with French."

From London the exhibition went to Berlin under the auspices of the Sturm Gallery. In Berlin all the remaining paintings were sold, but the exhibition, totaling thirty-four canvases, was kept together for subsequent showings in Brussels, Hamburg, Amsterdam, The Hague, Munich, Vienna, Budapest, Frankfort, Breslau, Wiesbaden, Zurich and Dresden. In the middle of the tour, the Futurists were invited to take part in the "Armory Show" in New York, held early in 1913, but they refused because they wanted separate galleries with a separate box office. Their work

11

was not to be shown in America until the San Francisco Exposition of 1915.

Boccioni did not accompany the exhibition on its grand tour, but returned from Berlin to Paris where he renewed his interest in sculpture. By the end of spring he had gone back to Milan in spite of Severini's insistence that all the Futurists should leave Italy to seek their artistic fortunes in the great competitive arena of the French capital. Marinetti, meanwhile, had gone east to enjoy the Balkan War which inspired his most famous poem, *Zang-tumb-tumb or The Siege of Adrianople.*

Back in Milan, the Futurists found that their international renown had not deeply impressed their fellow countrymen. Soffici, perhaps a little jealous of the Paris show, wrote another attack in *La Voce*, accusing the Futurists of charlatanism, professional vulgarity and of using Belgian and American publicity methods. Yet the article was kinder than the piece of a year before which had led to the battle of the Café Giubbe Rosse. Though he proclaimed that the Paris show was mostly a *succès de scandale*, he admitted that it had helped break down the legend of Italy's living in her cultural past. Severini, who had been introduced to Soffici by Picasso, now renewed their acquaintance in Tuscany, and before the end of the year a coalition between the Milanese and Florentine vanguards had taken place, thanks partly to Severini's diplomacy. Papini and Soffici actually deserted *La Voce* and founded a new magazine, *Lacerba*, which passed rapidly from tolerance of Futurism to enthusiastic participation. Thereafter, for a year and a half, *Lacerba* was the chief Futurist organ.

In February, 1913, the combined Milanese and Florentine forces put on an exhibition in Rome, and a Futurist Evening at the Costanzi Theatre where they were greeted with a "nutritious shower of missiles *più o meno alimentari*." The Roman exhibition, one of the best of all Futurist shows, included the mature work of Severini, the three Milanese and, for the first time, Balla and Soffici.

Boccioni showed six canvases including *Materia* (pl. 10), his major work of 1912, a complex painting in which the imposing figure of his mother, sitting with colossal folded hands, dominates, and at the same time is absorbed into her environment, the interior of the room, the window, the balcony and a row of houses across the street beyond. *Elasticity*, with its cantering horse and rider seen against a background of factories and high-tension poles, is less ambitious but better integrated (pl. 8).

Carrà's paintings of 1912 grew closer to the static analytical cubism of Picasso and Braque, though his Futurist masterpiece, *The Milan Galleria*, involves some suggestion of orthodox Futurist commotion (p. 127). The quality and restraint of Carrà's painting of this time quite belie the Futurist rebellion against "harmony" and "good taste." Soffici, the new recruit, also contributed work which seems more cubist than Futurist. Russolo showed *The Fog* (pl. 17), Balla, the *Girl × Balcony* and the *Leash in Motion* (pls. 26 and 25).

Balla, although he had signed the 1910 manifestoes, had developed his style in the comparative isolation of Rome. The *Girl × Balcony* shows that he had not yet freed himself from Signac-like neo-impressionist spot painting. The study for the feet in the *Girl × Balcony* suggests that his technique of kinetic suggestion is derived directly from the "geometrical chronophotographs" of figures in motion such as were made by E. J. Marey in Paris as early as 1883 and widely publicized. Balla's kinetic researches are clarified in the *Leash in Motion*, one of the most famous, original and entertaining of all Futurist paintings.

Among Severini's six pictures was his masterwork, the *Dynamic Hieroglyphic of the Bal Tabarin*, painted in Faenza in the summer of 1912 (pl. 22). In it are still a few passages which seem naïve and out of style, but on the whole the *Bal Tabarin* wonderfully assimilates and expresses the tinsel whirl of a Paris cabaret. The sequins glued to the canvas, Severini writes, had a respectable precedent in the jewel-encrusted halo of a fourteenth-century Saint Peter in the Brera, which Apollinaire mentioned to him. Severini's sequins themselves may have anticipated cubist collages by several months. Two years before, however, the cubists had begun to use isolated words and letters in their compositions. Severini, of course, knew their work but with typically Futurist concern for subject matter he scatters such words as VALSE, BOWLING, POLKA through his *Bal Tabarin* as integral and positive elements in the representation of the scene. Later, words and images are used in almost equal balance by Severini and Carrà in some of their war pictures and by Marinetti in his war poems.

The exhibition in Rome marks a high point in the development of Futurist painting, indeed of Futurism as an art movement. The show traveled as a whole to Rotterdam and selections from it were shown in Berlin and elsewhere, including Balla's *Leash in Motion* and Severini's *Bal Tabarin* which was sold in London. Many young artists of talent and some older men were attracted to the Futurist standard, and Futurism's influence grew stronger throughout Europe. Even the French critics and artists were now not only more respectful, they even borrowed Futurist critical and pictorial ideas, usually without giving credit. All through 1913 *Lacerba*'s pages were full of new manifestoes and polemical articles by Boccioni, Carrà, Marinetti, Soffici and Papini. Russolo published his manifesto on the *Futurist Art of Noises* and followed it with performances on his noise-machine in Paris and London as well as in Italy. Pratella, whose manifesto of Futurist music had appeared in 1910, conducted a Futurist symphony in Rome. Carrà was asked by Diaghilew and Strawinsky to design a ballet. Severini had a successful one-man show in London. Most important of all, Boccioni held his first exhibition of Futurist sculpture in Paris. The Futurists staged violent evenings at Genoa, Venice, Mantua, Padua, the series coming to a climax in Florence on December 12 at the Teatro Verdi where Carrà's "smoking" was soiled by a direct hit of *"pasta asciutta."*

Among the memorable Futurist paintings of 1913 are Severini's train compositions, of which the large drawing, plate 21, is an effective example. The use of chevron or wedge-shaped forms to suggest speed and force had however been initiated by Russolo in 1911 in his striking *Revolt*

(p. 133). Throughout 1913 Balla also experimented successfully with the suggestion of speed in a series of automobile pictures which began with the earlier *Speeding Automobile* (pl. 29). Balla's *Swifts*, sub-titled *Paths of Movement + Dynamic Sequences*, combines exterior and interior, moving and static objects by fusing kinetic series of birds in flight with the window frame and suggestions of roof tiles and gutters. (pls. 27 and 28).

Boccioni painted the *Dynamism of a Cyclist*, a study for which is reproduced on page 126, and the *Dynamism of a Human Body*. To these may be added the best known of his drawings, *Muscular Dynamism* (pl. 16). These three pictures belong fundamentally to the long series of studies of the human figure in action, striding, running, cycling, which pre-occupied Boccioni more than any other subject. In painting, these researches are climaxed by the huge *Football Player* of 1913. More notable, however, than any of these pictures is the series of striding figures in sculpture which he completed in the same year.

Boccioni's theories of sculpture, announced in the *Technical Manifesto of Futurist Sculpture*, April 11, 1912, were just as elaborate as his painting theories. They were also more prophetic of future developments, far more than he himself could realize in his two short years of work as a sculptor. In the manifesto he condemns, of course, the oppressive weight of the Greeks and Michelangelo upon the contemporary sculpture of France, Belgium and Italy. He scorns the archaistic and primitivist tendencies in Central European sculpture. He rejects the academic insistence upon the nude human figure and proposes sculpture which would integrate the complex elements and emotions of contemporary life. He dismisses his older contemporaries Meunier, Bourdelle, Rodin, but praises with real sympathy the plastic fluidity and freedom of Medardo Rosso. He proposes a sculpture of movement and atmosphere, the abolition of the silhouette, the extension of natural forms into space and the use of *polimateria*, that is, the abandonment of the traditionally "noble" materials of bronze and marble for glass, wood, cardboard, concrete, horsehair, leather, cloth, mirrors, electric lights, in various combinations. He foresees sculpture not only of forms in movement but sculpture itself mechanically mobile.

Boccioni's own sculpture falls into two periods, before and after his visits to Paris in the winter of 1911-12. The early work is ambitiously complex. *Head+House+Light*, now destroyed, was very closely related to the painting *Materia* (pl. 10), but the fusion of the woman's figure with a balcony and a house across the street together with rays of light result in a grotesque conglomeration, courageous but too doctrinaire. In Paris in March of 1912 Severini had taken him to the studios of Archipenko, Brancusi and Duchamp-Villon. Although his own ideas were more radical than theirs, their more traditional and less pictorial sculpture may have persuaded Boccioni to return to more manageable problems.

Back in Milan, he began the series of striding figures. The first, *Synthesis of the Human Dynamism*, still includes miscellaneous fragments of environment such as window mullions. In 1913 he abandoned these accessories, clarifying his forms in three successive figures, the *Spiral Expansion of Muscles in Movement*, the *Muscles in Velocity* and the climactic *Unique Forms of Continuity in Space* (pl. 13). This last figure well embodies Boccioni's theory that "sculpture should bring to life the object by making visible its prolongation into space. The circumscribed lines of the enclosed statue should be abolished. The figure must be opened up and fused in space." The muscles of the *Continuity* figure are forced into streamlined shapes as if under the distorting pressure of supersonic speed. The sense of gravity is further diminished by the flaming spiral of the figure when seen from the front.

A still life of 1912, the *Development of a Bottle in Space* (pl. 12), demonstrates Boccioni's dictum that "there is more truth in the intersection of the planes of a book with the corners of a table . . . than in all the twisting of muscles in all the breasts and thighs of the heroes and venuses which inspired the idiotic sculpture of our time."

Boccioni took his ten pieces of sculpture and twenty drawings to Paris for a show at the Galerie

La Boëtie in June, 1913. At the opening he spoke in faltering French which Severini helped to interpret to an audience more sympathetic and respectful than that which had greeted Marinetti at the general exhibition of Futurist painting fifteen months before. Though influenced somewhat by cubism, the two works here illustrated seem more advanced than any sculpture of the period in which they were done; and the *Continuità* remains one of the brilliant achievements of early twentieth-century art.

Futurism as a movement continued to gain ground in Italy during 1914. Adding still another art to the movement, the architect Antonio Sant' Elia published his manifesto *L'Architettura Futurista* in *Lacerba* of August 1, 1914, together with remarkably prophetic projects for skyscrapers with terraced setbacks several years before the zoning law brought about similar designs in New York. And Boccioni published his *Pittura, Scultura Futuriste*, the authoritative source-book on early Futurist art.

In his paintings Boccioni, abandoning the expression of violent movement, worked on the traditional theme of the figure seated at a café table, adding light rays and psychological atmosphere which were lacking in cubist paintings of similar subjects (pl. 14). Severini began a series of highly abstract compositions painted in a whirl of gay, rainbow colors, among them the *Dancer—Helix—Sea* (pl. 24). Carrà and Soffici, however, were more and more influenced by cubism. They assimilated collage techniques with greater skill and sensibility than any but the best Paris cubists (pl. 30). Indeed Carrà recalls that in the spring of 1914 he was offered a contract by Kahnweiler, discriminating dealer of Picasso, Braque and Gris.

The outbreak of the European war in August, 1914, aroused the Futurists to even more violent activity. Boccioni had written in the catalog of the Paris exhibition of February, 1912, "If our paintings are Futurist, it is because they represent the result of ethical, esthetic, political and social concepts which are absolutely Futurist." To the faithful, Futurism was a way of life devoted, among other things, to the patriotic aggrandizement of Italy. The Futurists were anti-German and, of course, anti-Austrian. They were pro-French politically and through strong personal associations, particularly in the cases of Marinetti, Soffici and Severini. Consequently they threw themselves with the utmost energy and enthusiasm into the cause of Italian intervention on the side of the Allies. As a result of public demonstrations, they were several times arrested and jailed (once with Mussolini, in Rome) and when Italy finally entered the war in April, 1915, most of the Futurists responded wholeheartedly and courageously to the call to arms. Russolo and Boccioni enlisted in the artillery. Marinetti was wounded and twice decorated. Sant' Elia was killed.

Boccioni's letters from the front reveal the natural conflict between Futurist romanticism and military reality. To Vico Baer he writes: "At last I have received the baptism of fire . . . I counted seventeen shots, four explosions a few steps away which covered us with leaves and earth. Fortunately Marinetti and I were flat on the ground." And again, "Here we are fighting against the wind, the hard rocks and the bugs. Excuse me, it is hard to believe it, but war is made up also of this: bugs, boredom and unsung heroism." But he could also write with true Futurist *élan:* "We have been shelling for four days to open the road . . . it is marvelous. 149 shells going over like express trains. It is beautiful and terrible. Tomorrow we move forward. I shall write you. At least I hope to. . . ."

But, on that tomorrow or perhaps a little later, Boccioni was hit and invalided to a base hospital at Verona. There, one day in the summer of 1916, before he was fully recovered, and under circumstances of extreme romantic irony, he was killed in a riding accident.

"The War is a motor for art," Carrà proclaimed in his book *Guerrapittura* published in 1915 and signed Carrrà``—with one extra consonant, two extra accents and a growl. And between political demonstrations and military service, the Milanese Futurists produced a number of drawings such as Carrà's *Cannon at a Gallop* or Boccioni's *Charge of Lancers,* brushed on a collage of war news clippings (pl. 15). But it was Severini who made the best Futurist pictures of the war, perhaps because he took no active part in it. During 1915 he lived near a station on the outskirts of Paris where he could see ammunition and Red Cross trains moving to and from the front. The *Armored Train* was probably painted at this time (pl. 23). The drawing, *Flying over Rheims,* must be one of the first air-view pictures by a well-known modern artist. Earlier in his life Severini had wanted to be an aviator. (See page 134.)

Yet, in spite of the stimulation of the War, the original group of Futurist artists was disintegrating. By the end of 1914, Boccioni had begun to desert Futurism for a more static and traditional technique. His last important work, the portrait of his friend the great pianist Busoni, was completed in 1916 not long before his death, in a style very close to Cézanne. Carrà's ardor as a Futurist painter was also cooling. In 1915 he forsook Futurism in his painting; in 1916 he contributed articles in praise of Giotto and Uccello to *La Voce* which had revived as a rival to *Lacerba;* and early in 1917 he became a collaborator of de Chirico in *pittura metafisica,* a movement entirely anti-Futurist in spirit. In 1915, Papini, the publisher of *Lacerba,* and Soffici, too, formally repudiated Futurism, going back, as Marinetti scornfully expressed it, to "*passatismo.*" However, Balla remained faithful; and Rosai and then Sironi, whose later works are reproduced in plates 68 and 83, joined the movement briefly. In Paris, after his Futurist war pictures of 1915, Severini accompanied Picasso back to a kind of neo-classic style, at least in his figure painting. It is true that as late as 1917, Carrà and Severini signed themselves as Futurists in one-man shows, the former in Milan, the latter in Alfred Stieglitz' Gallery in New York. But their allegiance was vestigial. When Marinetti emerged from the war to ally himself with his fellow interventionist, Mussolini, none of the original band of artists was with him save only Balla.

Futurism undoubtedly involved some of the same elements as Fascism: chauvinism for instance, admiration for war and military courage, enthusiasm for technology and machinery—"modernolatry"—to use Boccioni's word. But, fundamentally, Futurism was anarchic, not Fascist. Once Fascism was in power, the love of freedom, of perpetual revolt against the stale and conventional which had characterized early Futurism, was no longer politically valuable within the discipline of the totalitarian state. A second generation of Futurists grew up around Marinetti, painted, wrote manifestoes, demonstrated and were accorded some official recognition. A few of them were men of talent but their activities seem marginal and their achievements minor in quality beside those of the original Futurists. More congenial to the Fascist régime—and far better rewarded by it—were the *Novecentisti* who, as Mr. Soby recounts, rode the general wave of reaction and isolationism by painting old-masterish figures and landscapes, often with solemn references to the Italian Renaissance or Imperial Rome.

Throughout Europe, however, the influence of early Futurism was perhaps greater than that of any movement save cubism. Often dismissed by the French as a rather tasteless and provincial back eddy of cubism, Futurism was in principle, a repudiation of the static, puristic and quasi-academic elements in the Paris movement. Quite deliberately Boccioni insisted upon the importance of subject matter and overt emotion which the *fauve* and cubist movements had almost eliminated in favor of an art of pure esthetic values. A number of Paris artists and critics felt the impact of Futurism. In 1913 Apollinaire himself contributed a manifesto, *L'Antitradizione Futurista*, to *Lacerba*. And the Dadaists of 1916 turned to the Futurists for valuable precedent in iconoclastic agitation and as well for their later rejection of the dogmas of the *Section d'Or* cubists. Through the Dadaists, the irrational element in Futurism passed on to Paris Surrealism in the early 1920's. Futurism also influenced the Berlin *Sturm* group before 1915, the Berlin Dadaists such as George Grosz after 1917, the British Vorticists of 1914, the Central European Activists, and Americans such as Weber and Stella.

Marinetti had lectured in Moscow in 1914 and it was in Russia both before and after the Revolutions of 1917 that Futurism flourished most vigorously. The kinetic effects in Malevich's painting of 1912-13 anb later in the work of Burliuk, the dynamic-mechanical, multimaterial esthetics of Tatlin's constructions, the general machinolatry of the theatre, the poetry of Mayakovsky, all were in large part latently or avowedly Futurist in inspiration. But Futurism soon shared the fate of other modern movements in the U.S.S.R. As in Nazi Germany ten years later, they were discouraged and then suppressed by a regime which feared any sign of individual freedom or of nonconformity with popular taste as exploited by authoritarian politicians.

The year 1949 marks the fortieth anniversary of Italian Futurism. Conceived in a spirit of cultural rebellion, born as an instrument of international rivalry, nourished in the rumor of war, discolored by subsequent political associations, Futurism and its works are not easy to appraise. Even its name or, rather, the adjective "futuristic," has been misapplied by the general public to almost everything new and modern that has emerged in the art of the past four decades. Yet it should be possible now to wipe the dust of age and battle from these paintings and drawings and sculptures and look at them with fresh interest and a certain objectivity. However we may ultimately judge the quality of their work and whatever mischievous ideas we may deplore in their doctrine, we may conclude that few ventures in the history of art have been conducted with more energy, courage, and enthusiasm than that of the early Futurists.

The writer wishes to thank Donna Benedetta Marinetti for permission to examine her late husband's scrapbooks; Vico Baer for making accessible his letters from Boccioni; Romeo Toninelli and Raffaele Carrieri for making available the photographs assembled for the latter's important unpublished book on Futurism; and Miss Margaret Scolari for her translations of Italian texts. Other valuable sources have been the memoirs of Carrà (bibl. 112) and Severini (bibl. 241); Rosa Trillo Clough's Looking Back on Futurism *(bibl. 76), an excellent study of the literature and criticism; and Boccioni's* Pittura, Scultura Futuriste *(bibl. 91).* A. H. B., JR.

The Scuola Metafisica

"Metaphysical painting was more a way of seeing than a formal school," Alberto Savinio has told the writer in describing the *scuola metafisica* of which his brother, Giorgio de Chirico, was the founder and leading figure. The school's aim in brief was to portray an imagery intensified by philosophical reverie, to convey a sense of enigma through an evocative juxtaposition of objects in "unreal" settings, as in the pictures reproduced (pls. 31 to 41). Unlike Futurism, *pittura metafisica* had no inaugural program, nor did it result in a widespread group activity. Yet the fact remains that it is a distinguishable movement in modern art which evolved as follows.

In January, 1917, the painter Carlo Carrà was sent as a soldier to Ferrara, where de Chirico had been stationed for sixteen months or more. The two men became friends in the military hospital to which both were assigned because of nervous disorders, and from their association developed the *scuola metafisica*, which was fundamentally a rationalization of the art de Chirico had been creating in Paris from 1912 to 1915, as will appear. The two painters' association was extremely brief. Early in the summer of 1917 Carrà was given convalescent leave and returned to Milan, where he organized an exhibition of his pictures at the Chini Gallery (Dec. 18, 1917-Jan. 10, 1918). De Chirico, however, remained at Ferrara until he was demobilized in the winter of 1918-19.

Also in the hospital at Ferrara were Savinio, then a writer and musical composer, and Filippo de Pisis, writer and painter. Savinio's role as literary and philosophical adviser to the *scuola metafisica* may well have been important. But de Pisis' persistent claim to a major role is invalidated by his youth and inexperience as a painter at that time. In 1917 de Pisis was twenty-one and had painted little, while Carrà, at thirty-six, was a veteran of the entire Futurist campaign. De Chirico, though only twenty-nine, had a brilliant career in Paris behind him, and had been called "the most astonishing painter of the young generation" by Guillaume Apollinaire.

If the two chief protagonists of "metaphysical" painting were unquestionably de Chirico and Carrà, the movement included a third important artist. This was Giorgio Morandi of Bologna. Morandi, however, was never at Ferrara with the other two painters, and did not take part in their movement until 1918, when his own research took him in a comparable direction. He had met Carrà at a Futurist gathering at Bologna in 1912, but the two men did not become friendly until 1919, and Morandi says he did not see any of Carrà's "metaphysical" pictures until 1923, though he had known some of them in reproduction since 1918. He first knew de Chirico and his paintings in 1919. By that time de Chirico had abandoned *pittura metafisica* for a conscious emulation of late Renaissance precedent. Indeed, it is interesting that Morandi remembers seeing de Chirico for the first time at the Galleria Borghese in Rome, where the latter was copying a portrait by Lorenzo Lotto. According to de Chirico's autobiography, it was at this time, and in that museum, that he decided on a return to tradition—"that I had a revelation of great painting."

If de Chirico was the first to desert the *scuola metafisica* (he revived his Ferrarese iconography at intervals for a number of years, but in a different spirit), he was followed by Morandi at the end of 1920 and by Carrà late in 1921. But the school's brief cohesive character as a group manifestation began to disintegrate in 1919, due to a growing enmity between its two principal figures. In that year Carrà published a collection of his essays in a book entitled *Pittura Metafisica*, though only a single chapter dealt directly with the subject at hand. The book was adversely reviewed by de Chirico in 1920. Since the latter was without question the inventor of "metaphysical" painting, he may well have been irritated that his disciple had rushed its premise into print. And Carrà

17

appears to have had a more persuasive voice than de Chirico in the editing of Mario Broglio's magazine, *Valori Plastici* (1918-21). This magazine brought the *scuola metafisica* international fame, and extended its influence beyond the few years of its active course.

So much for the dramatis personae of the movement and for the dates of its existence. We must now consider separately the careers which in combination gave the school its identity.

GIORGIO DE CHIRICO

De Chirico was born in Greece of Italian parents. His father was an engineer for railroad lines then being constructed, and there can be little doubt that the painter's persistent iconographic use of draftsman's instruments and trains refers back to childhood memory of the elder de Chirico's profession. Giorgio showed talent in drawing at an early age, and was tutored in Athens and Volo by a series of local artists whose names and capacities he has listed in his recent autobiography. Eventually he studied drawing for four years at the Polytechnic Institute at Athens, and experimented with oil painting at home. After the death of his father, his mother decided to take her sons back to Italy. But presently she moved with them to Munich, where de Chirico could study art and the younger boy, soon known professionally as Alberto Savinio, music.

At Munich de Chirico enrolled in the Academy of Fine Arts, thus adding to what was already an exceptionally thorough technical training. Yet it was outside the Academy that he found his main inspiration—in the painting of Arnold Böcklin. More adept at languages than his brother, he would accompany Savinio to the latter's music lessons—"When I did not have to translate into Italian the professor's remarks, I would leaf through a large album of magnificent prints of Böcklin's paintings." Böcklin's influence was to persist throughout de Chirico's early period (1911-17), though in dwindling degree, and accounts in good measure for its emphasis on supernatural as opposed to sensory mood. Mention must also be made of de Chirico's youthful enthusiasm for Gustav Klimt, Max Klinger and Alfred Kubin. The last-named artist's print, *Vision of Italy*, parallels with striking fidelity de Chirico's images of vast, haunted squares, peopled by statues and drowned in silence.

The second great experience of de Chirico's years in Munich was his discovery of Friedrich Nietzsche's prose. In his autobiography the painter recalls what seems to him to have been Nietzsche's most impressive innovation: "This innovation is a strange and profound poetry, infinitely mysterious and solitary, based on *Stimmung* (which might be translated . . . as *atmosphere*), based, I say, on the *Stimmung* of an autumn afternoon when the weather is clear and the shadows are longer than in summer, for the sun is beginning to be lower." He adds: "the Italian city where this extraordinary phenomenon is most apparent is Turin." From Nietzsche's descriptions of deserted Italian squares came the basic inspiration for de Chirico's paintings of dream-lit piazzas, and it is a significant fact that he spent some time in Turin, on his way to Paris, just before this series began.

In 1909 de Chirico returned to Italy, where he painted several turbulent and romantic compositions in the style of Böcklin. In July, 1911, he followed his brother to Paris, where his mature career began. It began, however, less quickly than generally supposed. The first public exhibition in which he took part was the *Salon d'Automne* of 1912. Of his three accepted entries, the two most ambitious—*The Enigma of the Oracle* and *The Enigma of an Autumn Afternoon* are still so Böcklinesque, especially in color and in the conception of the figures, that they must rank as talented school pieces. Furthermore, his *Morning Meditation* of 1912, now in an Italian collection, is painted in a warm tonality of tan, rose and blue, indicating that he had not yet settled decisively on that hard, dry, thin, yet incalculably luminous technique which was to distinguish his works of 1913-14. His style attains full realization only with such pictures as the *Nostalgia of the Infinite* (pl. 31), whose inscribed date of 1911 is almost certainly false in view of the fact that it was first shown in the *Salon des Indépendants* of 1914, together with two works executed during the year preceding the *Salon's* opening.

De Chirico's paintings soon made a strong impression on a small but influential group of critics and artists, and won him the admiration of Guillaume Apollinaire, who is said to have contributed the mysterious titles of some of the painter's works. The French poet's enthusiasm for the young Italian—who was only twenty-five in 1913—is the more remarkable in that de Chirico's road ran counter to the direction of cubism, whose leading apologist was Apollinaire. To the cubists' frank acceptance of the canvas' two-dimensional limitations, de Chirico opposed a revival of extreme, illusory, linear perspective; in place of the rich and varied texture of Picasso's "Rococo" cubism of 1914, he used a bland, uniform surface, almost as meagre as a coat of priming, evoking an art of immense apparitional impact from an unassertive pigment. And what was far more important than any question of technical idiosyncracy, he substituted for the abstractionists' emphasis on formal and sensory order, an inner lyricism of mood and dream.

De Chirico's nightmare light and unreasonable shadows, his Renaissance towers and factory chimneys, his Victorian statues accosting the silence, his abandoned vans and ghostly trains, his figures dwarfed by labyrinthine arcades— these and other dramatic properties achieve an atmosphere of disquiet and omen, especially piercing in *The Mystery and Melancholy of a Street* (pl. 32). From his memories of Italian cities, particularly Florence and Turin, he created the series known collectively as the "memories of Italy," or the "piazzas of Italy." And it seems probable that homesickness gave his imagery a special intensity at this time. At least, if we include only those pictures in which architectural setting is the dominant theme, the series virtually ended with his return to Italy in 1915, though dubious paintings of a later date have appeared, and though de Chirico speaks in his autobiography of having painted at Ferrara in 1918 several *piazze d'Italia*, as well as pictures of mannequins and "metaphysical" still lifes.

The mannequin theme first appeared in de Chirico's art in 1914, while he was still in Paris. Raffaele Carrieri, seconded by Savinio himself, claims that the theme was suggested by Savinio's drama, *Les chants de la mi-mort*, which was published in Apollinaire's magazine, *Les soirées de Paris*, for July-August, 1914. The play's protagonist is a "man without voice, without eyes or face," and Savinio is said to have made a sketch for this figure which may have interested his brother as a plastic conception. At any rate, de Chirico soon began to include in his compositions draped, armless female figures, with the black outline of a single-eyed mask bound around their featureless heads. Presently these figures became male and female mannequins, clad in tights, with upholstered shoulders folded against their torsos like wings. In these pictures architecture functions merely as a backdrop to melancholy and ironic action by the mannequins. The series reaches its climax with the *Seer* (pl. 33), and takes on a new aspect in *The Disquieting Muses* of 1916 (color frontispiece), wherein the figures are hybrid sculpture-mannequin forms.

In certain 1913 paintings of Italian squares, de Chirico began to introduce still-life elements— fragments of plaster statuary, bananas, anatomical models, artichokes, pineapples—which despite their inanimate character, function as dramatic personages, stirring with an uncanny, allusive energy in a doomed and silent light. It seems likely, as Savinio has suggested, that the painter's interest in the symbolism of objects was inspired by Nietzsche's poetic animism, his insistence on the inner meaning of the commonplace and the "lifeless" when transposed from their normal setting. Yet de Chirico's symbols do not refer to an alternate reality, but are themselves a new and disturbing reality. Indeed to him may be applied Herbert Read's words on Paul Klee: " . . . the metaphysical painter seeks to find some plastic equivalent, not for the content of the thought, but for its felt intensity. The 'idea' is not illustrated: the illustration is the idea." And from de Chirico's 1913 use of disparate still-life accessories developed the third major subject of his early art—the "metaphysical still life," for which, at Ferrara, the *mise en scène* finally shifts from outdoors to indoors, from the broad piazza to the narrow room.

Sometime during the summer of 1915, de Chirico returned to Italy, was inducted into the Army, and was sent to Ferrara, where some of his finest works were executed. Even though he was confined much of the time to the military hospital, the painter was profoundly affected by the city in which he spent the war years, and he himself has described Ferrara's effect on his painting as follows: "The appearance of Ferrara, one of the loveliest cities in Italy, had made a deep impression on me, but what struck me above all and inspired me from the metaphysical point of view in which I was then working, was the appearance of certain interiors in Ferrara, certain window displays, certain shops, certain houses, certain quarters, as for instance the old ghetto where one could find candy and cookies in exceedingly strange and metaphysical shapes." The artist's mention of sweets and cookies is especially relevant, for these objects are portrayed in a majority of his Ferrarese still lifes. They probably appealed to him irresistibly at that time. His nervous breakdown was accompanied by a severe intestinal disorder of which a symptom is often an unreasonable longing for exotic and forbidden foods.

At Ferrara de Chirico abandoned the thin technique of his Paris period for a much heavier impasto, sometimes richly encrusted, as in the smoked whitefish of the *Sacred Fish* (pl. 35). Simultaneously his still lifes tended to become more crowded and more intricate in their directional weave. We do not know exactly what "shops," "houses" and "quarters" the painter saw on his walks through the city, nor can we be certain what effect his long confinement in the hospital had on his conception of space. But in his *Metaphysical Interior with Large Building* (pl. 34), the endless outdoor vistas of his Paris paintings appear only

in the picture-within-the-picture, that is, in the easel work in the center of the composition. Around this image are grouped various objects in an interior setting—triangles with baleful eyes, striped batons and unlikely armatures—while architecture is seen again through the open window. There results an unforgettable dislocation of everyday reality, a play back and forth between the near presence and a far dreaming. It would be an exaggeration, perhaps, to speak of de Chirico's Ferrarese still lifes as a "prison" art, yet some of them seem claustrophobic in their weight of descending forms, while in others the single window is distant and high.

The dramatization of still life remained one of de Chirico's principal concerns during his years at Ferrara. But his dramatic methods varied considerably. In the *Sacred Fish* (pl. 35), for example, the fish are placed like actors on a platform at the front of a stage, the principals of a drama of the inanimate. Their extreme realism is offset by the fantasy of the object near them and of the starfish impaled on a candlewick at the left—the known and the impossible combined to create a believable entity. It was this picture that came as a revelation to Max Ernst and other leaders of the Dada movement and soon established de Chirico as the leading, though recalcitrant, prophet of the surrealist uprising of 1924.

In *The Disquieting Muses* and *Grand Metaphysician* (frontispiece and pl. 36), de Chirico returned to the exterior settings of his *piazze d'Italia*, using as a backdrop in the former picture a recognizable image of the Castello Estense at Ferrara. But in both paintings, as in the *Seer* of two years before, the architecture is dominated by the presence of the figures: the elaborate still-life structure with mannequin head in the *Grand Metaphysician*, the menacing sculpture-mannequins of the *Muses*. Perhaps more forcefully than any other work of de Chirico's career, the *Muses* illustrates the ambivalent, "metaphysical" nature of his early art. The picture attracts and repels, beguiles and frightens, conveys a warm nostalgic aura but at the same time suggests an impending

20

catastrophe. There is no action; the piazza is still; the figures wait. What will happen? There is no answer, for this picture is the exact opposite of those seventeenth-century paintings of *banditti* in which a specific, disastrous outcome is foretold. De Chirico's image—his early art as a whole— appeals directly to the counter-logic of the sub-conscious, to those swamp-like regions at the edge of the mind where ecstasies bloom white and the roots of fear are cypress-black and deep.

CARLO CARRÀ

One of the five original Futurist artists, as has appeared, was Carlo Carrà, born in 1881 and therefore seven years older than de Chirico. To-ward the end of 1915 Carrà began to have serious reservations as to the validity of the Futurist premise. In particular he came to disbelieve in his colleagues' rebellious attitude toward native tra-dition. Whereas Boccioni, in an understandable attempt to throw off the oppressive weight of the Italian past, had once described Raphael as "disgusting," Michelangelo as "disgraceful," Carrà now found himself drawn irresistibly to the great masters. In 1915 he made a careful and enthusiastic study of Giotto's frescos. Inspired by their sim-plicity, warmth and grandeur, he completed the painting, *Lot's Daughters*, which ended his career as a wholehearted Futurist and later became a signpost to a quite general return to native heri-tage among modern Italian painters. In 1916 he published in *La Voce* two perceptive articles, *Parlata con Giotto*, and *Paolo Uccello, costruttore*. His part in the Futurist insurrection was over.

Carrà did not, however, abandon Futurism completely at this point, as is often claimed. From late 1915 until the end of 1917, according to his autobiography, "I still presented myself to the public as a dissident futurist, as may be seen from the catalog of my one-man show in Milan in 1917." His *Drunken Gentleman* (pl. 37), dated 1916 and almost certainly revised after that date, is inscribed on the back, "C. D. Carrà-futurista," though it is executed completely in the "meta-physical" style. Moreover, at intervals Carrà

revived elements of the cubist-Futurist technique, notably in his *Penelope* of 1917. Indeed he appar-ently hoped for a time to strike an equation be-tween what he described as two fundamental concerns of art—"statics and movement." This ambition, perhaps most graphically illustrated by *The Cavalier of the West* (pl. 38), proved difficult, and gradually the calm, monumental authority of his favorite medieval and Renaissance masters won out over Futurism's giddy kinetics. The ex-ample of Giotto and Uccello was soon reinforced by that of Masaccio and Piero della Francesca. By the close of 1915, his autobiography states, "I can affirm that I had the strongest desire to identify my painting with history, and especially with the history of Italian art." It is important to keep in mind Carrà's intense respect for the plastic solutions of his great predecessors, for this was the foundation of his approach to "metaphysical" painting, whereas de Chirico was able to say of Max Klinger: "the pictorial question did not matter, because his entire creation was based on the enormous possibilities of his exceptional mind —the mind of a poet, philosopher, observer, dreamer, scholar and psychologist."

In January, 1917, as previously stated, Carrà was assigned to the military hospital at Ferrara, and there joined forces with de Chirico to form the short-lived *scuola metafisica*. The two painters' backgrounds were extremely unlike. De Chirico, as we have seen, had been nourished by Germanic and predominantly philosophical sources, while Carrà was now immersed in the pictorial main-stream running from Giotto to Piero (when de Chirico finally turned to the Italianate tradition, it was to that of Raphael, Michelangelo, Dosso Dossi and Poussin, rather than to that of the earlier masters). The two men's only shared ex-perience was a first-hand knowledge of advanced developments in contemporary French art. As a Futurist Carrà had naturally been influenced by the cubists, while certain de Chirico paintings of 1913 indicate, in their angular spacing, that he, too, may have been obliquely affected by the Parisian abstractionists. But by 1917 or soon thereafter Carrà's interest focused on the *Douanier* Rousseau and on the leading French defender of tradition, André Derain; he included articles on the latter two artists in his *Pittura Metafisica* (1919), and published a monograph on Derain in 1921. De Chirico, for his part, had never been deeply absorbed in the School of Paris, and was willing to repudiate it entirely in favor of Böcklin, Klinger, Courbet and, presently, Raphael.

Considering their differences in training and taste, it is no wonder that Carrà's "metaphysical" painting is less like de Chirico's than generally supposed. As a partner in the *scuola metafisica* Carrà used a vocabulary of forms invented by de Chirico; there can be no doubt about that. Soon after his arrival in Ferrara, he took over from the latter such iconographical motifs as mannequin figures, engineering instruments, armatures, steep wooden flooring, children's toys, striped sticks, and so on. But he used this subject matter in a personal manner, and his dependence on de Chirico is less absolute than is suggested by one of his most widely reproduced pictures—the *Solitude* of 1917, so closely based on de Chirico's mannequin figures of 1915-17.

One of the cardinal points of emphasis in *pittura metafisica* was atmosphere, that is, the manipulation of texture, light and tone to create a mysterious ambiance for the enigmatic objects portrayed by the *scuola metafisica's* two principal artists. Carrà's handling of atmosphere was sensory, based on mid-fifteenth-century precedent, but striving as well for the emotional directness he admired in Giotto and Rousseau. His pictures were completed slowly (he painted only about fifteen "metaphysical" works in all, some of them drastically revised over a long period of time), and were built up layer by layer until they had a marked tactile appeal. De Chirico's texture by comparison is abstract and sophisticated, even if more assertive than during his Paris period.

A second ingredient of "metaphysical" atmosphere was light, and in its use the two artists again differed radically. Carrà's light is often an in-candescence, a soft inner radiance, supplemented by glowing reflections on the surface. This is perhaps especially true of later works such as *The Engineer's Mistress* (pl. 41), in which the figure appears to be dreaming in and of light, but even in the *Hermaphroditic Idol* of 1917 (pl. 40), a muted over-all illumination unifies the static, linear contours. In de Chirico's Ferrarese paintings, however, Carrà's diffused floodlighting tends to be replaced by dramatic spotlighting from the wings of the composition. His objects do not suggest translucence, as with Carrà, but are quite opaquely painted and thrown into relief by vigorous crosslighting or by abrupt changes in geometric form. Whereas de Chirico actually used a compass in painting the round epaulets of certain 1915 mannequins, it is difficult to think of Carrà as a mathematical precisionist. Instead the latter seems to have groped through his senses to a given vision, reassuring himself through almost scholastic reference to the art of the past. De Chirico, on the other hand, may well have experienced his subjects as total entities, like pressing hallucinations. His production was much more prolific than Carrà's because it was more immediate in conception.

In color Carrà made perhaps his most personal contribution to the *scuola metafisica*. While de Chirico's color is forceful and almost somber, as befits an art whose mood is ominous, that of Carrà is light, gracious, idyllic, at times allied to Piero's pale-sweet palette and nearly always recalling the mid-fifteenth-century fresco tradition. The pinks and grays of the latter's *Drunken Gentleman* are beguiling and tender; the sea greens and maroon of *The Engineer's Mistress* do not shock but soothe the eye. Moreover, during his "metaphysical" period Carrà explored a wide tonal range, progressing from the rainbow complexity of *The Cavalier of the West* to the almost monochromatic severity of the *Still Life with Triangle* (pl. 39). We cannot predict his color from black and white photographs, whereas de Chirico's art proceeds from so cohesive a vision that we very often know approximately what tones to expect.

This is not to say, of course, that the latter is a less subtle colorist than Carrà; he is indeed incomparably richer and more original.

With *The Engineer's Mistress*, Carrà's brief connection with the *scuola metafisica* came to an end. He is the only artist to have had a major role in the two principal movements of progressive art in modern Italy. To both movements he brought a remarkable sensitivity, a slow, tormented awareness, an ability to assimilate the discoveries of others and to add his own distinguishable program.

GIORGIO MORANDI

Morandi's activity in the *scuola metafisica* was peripheral, being carried on in the isolation of his studio at Bologna, as already noted. Born in that city and trained in its Academy of Fine Arts, he developed as a young man a profound admiration for Cézanne. For a long time, however, he knew the French master's work in reproduction only, and it seems likely that he was stirred most of all by Cézanne's solitary dedication to plastic research within a restricted iconographic range. An occasional Morandi landscape of 1912 utilizes Cézanne's proto-cubist handling of planes, while the influence of cubism itself is felt in a few works of the pre-war years. We know, too, that Morandi was attracted briefly by the Futurists' premise. In short he was well aware of current developments; the archaic elongations of his 1916 *Still Life* (pl. 57) are not the work of an uninformed or reactionary painter.

In 1918 Morandi returned to the uncomplicated lyricism of the *Flowers* (pl. 59), with its pale colors and sensitive brushwork. But that same year his art congealed into a more rigid and mechanical order, as in the *Still Life with Box and Ninepin* (pl. 42), and his "metaphysical" period began. By that time he had seen photographs of Carrà's recent paintings. One wonders most whether he had also seen Ozenfant's and Le Corbusier's *Après le cubisme*, published that year, which announced the emergence of the Purist movement in Paris. In any case, Morandi's "metaphysical" paintings of 1918-20 are in many respects more closely related to Purism than to the art produced at Ferrara by de Chirico and Carrà. They are, however, quite deeply modeled, whereas the French Purists used flat, contiguous forms and arabesque contours.

In 1918, too, Morandi adopted the mannequin theme so variously portrayed by his colleagues in the *scuola metafisica*. He appears to have done so, not so much because of the theme's psychological potential as because the rounded, polished forms of the mannequins could provide an appealing compositional element in his purist art, playing against the shapes of bottles and tables in a predominantly formal sequence (pl. 44). There is, in brief, a lack of supernaturalism and shock in Morandi's "metaphysical" art as a whole, as compared to de Chirico's and Carrà's. In its place there is a lucid plastic equation of which Cézanne, rather more than Giotto or Nietzsche, is the guiding star.

Amedeo Modigliani

Of all twentieth-century Italian artists the most famous, with the possible exception of de Chirico, is Modigliani, who first arrived in Paris in 1906, and there became a legendary figure, ill, handsome, alcoholic, greatly loved, doomed to early death. Perhaps there is a certain justice in the fact that the memory of his personality is as alive as that of his art. In an era which often tended to ignore figure painting or to abstract it, Modigliani's obsession was the human face, the human form. Did he ever complete a still life or a landscape? If so, these works would take a minor place in his art. When as a sculptor he turned to classic architectural precedent, the motifs he preferred, significantly, were the caryatid figure or the corbeled head (pls. 47 and 48).

The infinite variety of the human face and the sinuous contours of the female nude—these were his inescapable themes. But what is to be noted is that he achieved considerable variety within a relatively narrow subject matter and style. He was formed as a mature painter, in Paris, by the impact of Cézanne, African sculpture and the cubists; he never broke violently away from these sources, as men like Picasso were to do. Yet he remained unmistakably an Italian artist, harking back periodically to the primitives, Botticelli, the sixteenth-century Mannerists. It was out of the strength of his Italianism that he was able to make

his own contribution to the modern idiom of the School of Paris.

Modigliani's emotional register was rich and subtle. From the witty insouciance of the *Bride and Groom* (pl. 53) he could turn to the gentle pathos of *The Servant* (pl. 46), and from that to the elegant sensuality of the *Reclining Nude* (pl. 51). His color was arbitrary and structural rather than predominantly atmospheric, yet it often acted as a barometer of mood: bright and defiant (opposite), or somber and melancholy. It is line, however, that is the backbone of his art—that sharp, deft, summary line which affirms his Renaissance heritage (pls. 49 and 50). Like so many painters whose drawing is incisive, like, for example, Géricault, Degas and Picasso, he was attracted to sculpture, and in that medium his love of stylization is conveyed with exceptional clarity and force (pl. 48).

As a painter, sculptor and draftsman, Modigliani has retained an eminent place over the thirty years that have elapsed since he died. His death occurred in 1920. This was precisely the moment when many of his countrymen at home were entering a long period of reactionary artistic isolation, returning in a nationalistic spirit to those native sources of which Modigliani, as much and usually more brilliantly than they, had made such fruitful use as an exile in Paris.

MODIGLIANI: *Woman with a Necklace*, 1917. Oil on canvas, 36⅜ x 24¾". Collection Charles H. Worcester, Chicago. Not in the exhibition.

Painting and Sculpture since 1920

Later Work of de Chirico, Carrà and Morandi

After the collapse of the *scuola metafisica*, its three protagonists resumed their separate paths which had crossed so briefly. De Chirico, released from the Army during the winter of 1918-19, moved from Ferrara to Rome, and there announced his return to the classical tradition by painting *The Return of the Prodigal* in the spirit of Raphael. In 1919 he also completed several fine small still lifes in which his "metaphysical" fantasy was replaced by a sensory handling of unobtrusive subject matter. He now publicly urged on his fellow artists a "return to craftsmanship," a renewal of exactly those pictorial virtues which had once seemed to him of secondary importance compared to philosophical content. (Oddly enough, his articles on Böcklin and Klinger first appeared in 1920, though his own painting by then testified to quite different interests—the art of the early sixteenth century in Italy and of such anti-metaphysical artists as Courbet.) *The Return of the Prodigal* was followed by several ambitious romantic-classical portraits and, from 1920 to 1922, by the remarkable series known as the "Roman Villas" (pl. 55). The series was executed in tempera, a medium to which de Chirico had turned after copying Michelangelo's *Holy Family* in the Uffizi Gallery and after listening to the advice of a Russian painter-friend, Lochoff. The "Roman Villas" were succeeded by a group of romantic mythological pictures inspired, perhaps, by the memory of Dosso Dossi's paintings at Ferrara; among these *The Departure of the Knight Errant* is outstanding (pl. 54). Soon de Chirico's respect for the past had broadened to include even the Rubens-Delacroix version of the Baroque, as may be seen in the flowing handling of his *Hector and Andromache* (pl. 56).

In 1925 de Chirico returned to Paris. There he found himself acclaimed as the leading prophet of the surrealist movement in art, inaugurated the year before. For a very short time he appears to have accepted the role with enthusiasm; at least we know that during 1925 he often returned to the proto-surrealist subject matter of his Ferrarese period. But presently he quarreled violently with the leaders of surrealism. His irrepressible fantasy of vision continued to assert itself periodically, notably in his paintings of mannequin figures with torsos composed of architectural fragments. For the most part, however, he now worked in a neo-classical style, depicting a ruined and desolate Greece inhabited by wild horses. According to Savinio, the painter's new interest in the landscape of his childhood was aroused by the anthropological studies of Sir James George Frazer, though Picasso's neo-classicism of 1919-23 was probably a more direct stimulus. In any case de Chirico's art became more and more eclectic, more and more concerned with technical virtuosity. He was never again to revert consistently to the apparitional painting on which his fame rests so securely.

Carrà, too, continued the return to tradition which in his case had begun in 1915 and had been interrupted only in the matter of iconographical oddity by his "metaphysical" period. He became —he remains to this day—primarily an elegiac interpreter of the Italian scene, disciple of Giotto's medieval sobriety, of mid-fifteenth-century monumentality (especially with his figure pieces) and of the atmospheric naturalism of the nineteenth-century Lombard impressionists. Yet traces of the "metaphysical" program were slow in disappearing from his work. His *Morning at the Seaside* (pl. 63), for example, seems at first glance an impressionistic commentary on a coastal view, saturated with the salt air and pervasive light. But the image is presented within the framework of a calculated pictorial order, exemplified at its most extreme by the placing of the sawhorse (which also appears in *The Pine* of 1921) in relation to the triangular struts in the foreground which are repeated geometrically in the ships' rigging. In this picture the enigmatic, striped poles of Carrà's Ferrarese painting have become functional properties of the seaside. Nevertheless, even here may be felt the impetus of his earlier career: a deliberate emotional primitivism; an arbitrary tonal manipulation; an emphasis on prescient calm. And if in recent years Carrà has become more nearly an unequivocal realist, his later works are often imbued with a strong idyllicism.

The third member of the *scuola*, Giorgio Morandi, is today almost universally considered by the Italians to be their finest living painter and his fame, unlike that of many of his contemporaries, is based on the accomplishment of his later as well as his earlier career. In certain paintings of 1920, the rigid forms of his "metaphysical" period began to thaw, and he returned, through the gradual stages which have marked his career as a whole, to the softer contours and less geometric placing of his 1916-18 still lifes. Since then he has devoted himself, with immeasurable integrity, to research within a narrow iconographic range—still life and an occasional landscape. As a result, his art does not communicate well in reproduction; indeed its seeming monotony disappears only on prolonged and comparative examination of the paintings themselves. Once seen in number, however, Morandi's pictures assert a new, variable and convincing order, as do those of Piet Mondrian, his nearest modern counterpart in spirit though not in style. In representational as opposed to Mondrian's abstract terms, Morandi has undertaken a devout study of slight yet critical shifts in the weight of counterbalancing forms. To appreciate his art it is necessary to accept the validity of his conscience and aim, of that immense creative devotion which he applies to the solution of plastic matters. Consider, for example,

the tiny bottle at the right of his 1939 still life (color plate opposite). Its presence is the clue to the entire composition, and was probably arrived at after endless experiment and revision.

What is most remarkable about Morandi's art, however, is that its purism rarely entails a sacrifice of lyric intensity. Morandi does not respond to the pressure of outer events. Year after patient year he rearranges the bottles in his studio at Bologna or looks outside at the Emilian fields. But his inspiration burns steadily, and his art grows on the observer like the commonplaces of major poetry in which a truism becomes exactly true for the first time. His usual expressive instrument is color, sometimes restricted to subtle variations within a close over-all tonality, as in the blue *Still life* of 1937 (pl. 62), or again expanded to encompass fairly abstract contrasts of light and shade (color plate). He regulates his chiaroscuro with the architectonic concentration of a Poussin, and with only partial regard for the demands of reality. Yet color and luminosity are inseparably allied in his art, as they were with Chardin. He gives each object an atmospheric enclosure, so that his art is essentially poetic and revelatory rather than sensual and decorative. And color is not the only string to his bow. His prints (pl. 60) are among the finest produced by modern Italy, and are surprisingly varied in technique. Considering his cumulative achievement, his countrymen's high regard for him seems justified, though in terms of youthful brilliance and of world influence he cannot be compared to de Chirico and Modigliani.

The Novecento

With the collapse of Futurism in 1915 and of the *scuola metafisica* toward the end of 1921, Italian painting was left without an advance-guard movement of real importance. During the 1920's, a second generation of Futurists made their appearance, while Alberto Savinio (become a painter), Arturo Nathan and de Chirico himself revived certain aspects of the "metaphysical" premise.

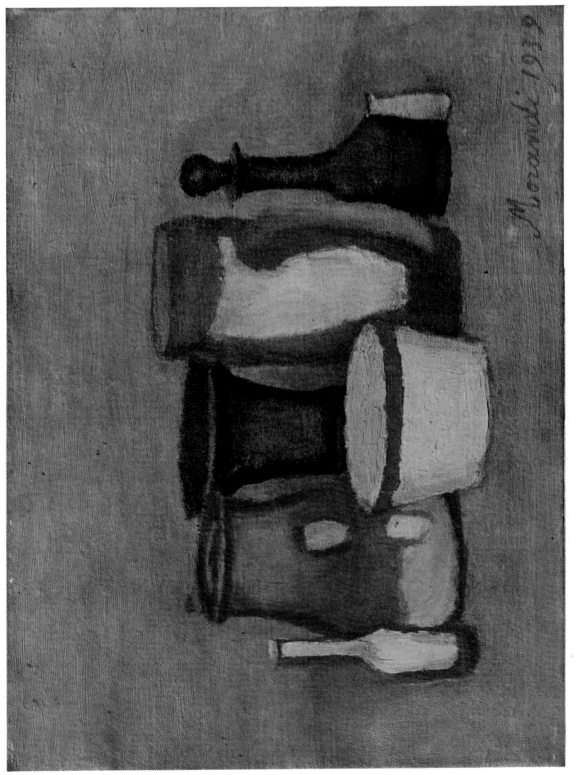

MORANDI: *Still Life*, 1939. Oil on canvas, 23½ x 31″. Collection Dr. Pietro Rollino, Rome.

Yet after the March on Rome, the influence of the two original movements was more effective outside Italy than in, since Futurism continued to contribute, if in diminishing degree, to a general European and American vocabulary of abstract forms, and the *scuola metafisica* led through de Chirico's painting to the surrealist movement in Paris. In Italy, on the contrary, there was a widespread impatience with insurrectionary developments in art, an impatience shared by de Chirico and Carrà, as we have seen. Indeed, the principal Italian school of the mid-1920's was the deliberately reactionary group known as the *Novecento*.

The *Novecento* came into existence with an exhibition at Milan organized by Margherita Sarfatti in the winter of 1926. It included at first only a small group of artists who were allied by a common faith in the need for an idealization of art's character and function. After the stormy years of cubism and Futurism, the *Novecento* proposed a revival of more traditional subjects and techniques; it hoped to recapture the inspirational solemnity of the great Italian past. Its program was unquestionably affected by the Fascist regime which, though it did not emulate the harsh Nazi persecution of "modern" artists until after the outbreak of the recent war, imposed a certain provincialism on Italian painters by officially rewarding their more chauvinistic efforts and by discouraging cultural ties with the outside world. The *Novecento*'s most assertive facet was perhaps the rather pompous neo-classicism of Achille Funi, Piero Marussig and others. Gradually, however, the movement became merely a convenient grouping of those Italian artists who were leaving in abeyance the troubling international developments of earlier twentieth-century art, returning not only to classical precedent but to the comparative realism of the nineteenth century. If at the one extreme of the *Novecento* was neo-classic allegory, at the other was the anti-rhetorical impressionism of men like Arturo Tosi and Pio Semeghini.

Tosi, who lives at Milan, is the dean of living Italian painters. His art parallels in Lombard terms the French intimism of Pierre Bonnard, though it avoids the latter's compositional intricacies. Tosi's lyric response to familiar subjects is notable for its quiet immediacy (pls. 64 and 65); its roots are in the tonal preoccupations of the French and especially the Lombard impressionists.

Another older artist of Milan is PIO SEMEGHINI, who has developed a modest and appealing version of the Rococo tradition. His deft, reticent technique allies him, like Tosi, to the less doctrinaire aspects of impressionism. But his palette reveals a special sympathy for the eighteenth century's lucid, nursery colors, perhaps above all for those of Jean Etienne Liotard, whose works Semeghini would have known during his long residence in Switzerland.

Also at Milan is the much younger MARIO SIRONI, who may have inherited from Boccioni an interest in modern industrial subject matter (pl. 68). To the *Novecento* Sironi brought a powerful romantic expressionism which seems to have been developed independently, being as closely related to the seventeenth-century Italian Baroque as to the art of Rouault. Sironi's sometimes turbulent vision is today expressed with unrelaxed vigor in such pictures as *The Flagellation* (pl. 70). He occupies a solitary position among modern Italian artists. His expressionism is often focused on subjects which are in themselves dramatic, whereas with the exception of Scipione his countrymen's art in this vein usually emulates Soutine's passionate analysis of dispassionate themes. But Sironi's art has another side: an archaic formalism, the result perhaps of his earlier preoccupation with large-scale fresco and mosaic decorations. During the past fifteen years he has completed a number of pictographic compositions (pl. 69), in which his usual Lombard vehemence is splintered and restrained.

The painting of FELICE CASORATI of Turin is a totally different matter. Over the years Casorati has evolved a calm, studio art of which the nude figure is a principal subject. Within a purposely "artificial" ambiance, his figures have a memorable and not at all stilted poignancy. Of all living artists he and the younger French artist, Balthus, may have most tellingly depicted the angular uncertainties of adolescence. But whereas Balthus dwells on psychological innuendo, Casorati concentrates on a physical, almost Mannerist tension of pose. The admirer of such disparate artists as Masaccio, Uccello, Georges de La Tour and Ingres, Casorati is a stern classicist with the temperament of a romantic, not unrelated to the modern German painter, Karl Hofer. His art conveys so strong a sense of pedagogical research that its expressive drawing tends at first to go unnoticed. But the line which underlies his blond and circumspect art is swift and bold. It is no accident that de La Tour no less than Vermeer or Ingres is a pillar of his esthetic.

The Middle Generation

Whereas Casorati has spent nearly all of his career in Italy, MASSIMO CAMPIGLI of the slightly younger generation is one of the few modern Italian artists who have usually worked abroad. From 1919 until the recent war, Campigli lived mostly in Paris, exhibiting there and in New York. And Paris had much to do with his evolution as a painter. Indeed, he himself has listed as three main formative influences the neo-classicism of Picasso, the cylindrical forms of Léger's painting in the early 1920's and, above all, the stylized, corseted figures and parasols of Seurat. Yet Campigli's art has remained unmistakably Italian, explicable first of all in relation to Etruscan and Pompeian classicism. We know, too, that it was Italy which taught him to make effective use of his French enthusiasms. Returning to Italy for a visit in 1928, he was awakened as an artist by an excited study of the Etruscan Museum at the Villa Giulia in Rome. His mature career began almost at once. From the sculpture in the Villa Giulia he developed the rounded, compartmented style which established him as a new personality in modern Italian painting (pl. 71). Since that

early day Campigli's art has become more subtle in color, and his system of close-up fragmentation has been extended to include such ambitious and inventive compositions as *The Staircase* (pl. 74). His archaism has always had a decided contemporary liveliness, as in *The Garden* with its assimilated references to Seurat's schematism and to the chalky harmonies of Renaissance fresco.

A contemporary of Campigli and a fellow-expatriate in Paris is FILIPPO DE PISIS, an extremely different temperament, advocate of the bright, quick phrase rather than of the balanced metaphor. Indeed, in de Pisis' art spontaneity becomes an irresistible, impulsive principle. Prolific to the point of carelessness, his work often resembles, as Delacroix said of Victor Hugo, "the rough draft of a man of talent; he says everything that comes into his head." Nevertheless, de Pisis has produced a number of fine paintings which have won him a deserved international recognition. His early *Napoleon's Horse* and *Still Life with Funnel and Shopping Bag* (pl. 77) suggest Manet in their bravura and easy solidity, while a certain fantasy of assembly in the objects is probably due to the artist's association with de Chirico's *scuola metafisica*. Presently, however, de Pisis adopted a much looser technique, as in the *Poultry Yard* (pl. 78), with its casual accents and impatient eloquence. Working at great speed, the artist has sought to record his instantaneous sensibility toward subjects which range from vegetables and seashells to the Baroque architecture of Venice, where he has often worked. In short de Pisis might be described as a romantic impressionist. Yet despite his long residence abroad and his debt to Manet's circle, he has remained, like Campigli, a thoroughly Italian artist, descendant of the eighteenth century's Francesco Guardi in flecked color and staccato line. Because he improvises with such rapt faith in his own virtuosity, he succeeds or fails according to the clarity and depth of the emotion that prompts a given work. His lack of meditative integrity is his vice—and his virtue.

Two artists who have developed in separate

directions since their association with the broad ideals of the later *Novecento* are VIRGILIO GUIDI and POMPEO BORRA. During the decade preceding the second World War, Guidi alternated between an impressionist landscape technique, with close French affiliations, and a neo-classic but sometimes realistic figure style. Very recently, like many Italian painters, he has turned to abstraction, working in a manner which recalls the rounded simplifications of Germany's Oskar Schlemmer but is exceptionally pungent in color (pl. 76). Borra, on the other hand, has abandoned the abstract purism with which he experimented at times during the 1930's, and has returned to the enthusiasm of his earliest professional years: mid-fifteenth-century humanism, especially that of Piero della Francesca. Today Borra applies his neo-classicism to subjects of current humanitarian significance, as in the *Refugees* (pl. 81), and also to those of an idealistic detachment, as in the *Concert for Two Flutes* (pl. 80). But unlike so many modern artists who have fallen under Piero's spell, he has retained his own sincerity, whose safeguard is a touching, shy humility.

Two Realists: Rosai and Donghi

Until recently twentieth-century Italian painting has seldom been concerned with social realism, and even today the political commentary of men like Guttuso (opp. p. 32) and Pizzinato (pl. 113) is communicated in relatively abstract terms. There is, however, a notable exception to this generality: the art of OTTONE ROSAI of Florence. After training briefly at the Institute of Decorative Art and at the Academy of Fine Arts in that city, Rosai joined the Futurist movement, being particularly affected by the cubist-Futurist pictures of Ardengo Soffici (pl. 30). His career was interrupted by long service in the first World War, and when he returned home he decided on a new direction for his painting. Was he at this point converted to a more representational approach by the frescos of Giotto, as Carrà had been before him? At any rate, Rosai in 1919 painted several small

still lifes (pl. 84), in which the plastic isolation of the objects against a uniform ground suggests *trecento* still lifes.

Perhaps it was the overpowering vitality of fourteenth-century realism that persuaded Rosai to abandon Futurist abstraction for an opposite course. From 1919 to 1922 he painted a number of small pictures of street scenes in Florence, showing with extreme acuteness of characterization the life of the working people (pl. 83). He has retained the same subject matter to this day, though his increasing emphasis on impressionistic atmosphere has tended to soften the edge of his social observation, and he has painted "pure" landscapes more frequently than before. But his little genre scenes of the early 1920's, paralleling in a less satirical mood the art of our own Ben Shahn and of the Mexican Antonio Ruiz, are admirable works, forceful, handsomely painted, and quite exceptional in modern Italian painting as a whole.

The realism of ANTONIO DONGHI, on the other hand, has nothing to do with politico-social commentary. It proceeds from an earnest, almost pious longing for the maximum clarity and order. Indeed, his reverence for the illusionistic powers of his craft reminds us of the *Douanier* Rousseau, and many of his pictures seem "primitive" in their awed directness and lack of sophistication. But Donghi reminds us, too, of Cranach and Ingres, as the Italian critic Leonardo Sinisgalli has pointed out, and several of his compositions owe much to Seurat, whose pointillism is immeasurably remote from Donghi's sharp-focus technique. This latter technique, however, is controlled by a cautious plastic balance, like a frozen Mannerism. The result, in Donghi's art, is a curious, static dignity. *The Hunter* (pl. 82), for example, is a snapshot which becomes a medallion, a portrait but also a quasi allegory. The striding, mustachioed man is made almost emblematic by the presence of the boy, with falconer's pole, who might be the standard bearer for a more momentous excursion. Yet at other times, especially in his works of the early 1930's, Donghi becomes a straight-forward recorder of everyday events. His *Departure* is a document such as might be preserved in a family album. It belongs to the realm of art not so much because of Donghi's technical precision as because of his dogged warmth as a painter.

The Roman School

If Milan offers by far the most active market for contemporary Italian art, some of the leading painters born in the 1890's continue to work at Rome. Among them is LUIGI BARTOLINI, whose etchings are eloquent, personal and impressive (pls. 87 and 88), and FAUSTO PIRANDELLO, son of the playwright, whose sensual enjoyment of his medium calls Braque to mind. Pirandello's encrusted surfaces belong to the decorative side of expressionism. His seems basically a "private" art, an art of slow relish and marked poetic absorption (pl. 89).

It was in Rome, too, that the first successful resistance to the authority of the *Novecento* developed. This was the so-called "Roman School" of SCIPIONE (Gino Bonichi) and MARIO MAFAI, both born soon after the turn of the century. To the ponderous classicism of the *Novecento* the two young painters opposed an impulsive neo-romanticism, finding their subjects not in the perorations resounding from the Fascist Olympus, but in the a-political and human sound of the city. Whereas many artists of the older generation had adopted a life of professorial when not of official pomp, the "Roman School" created a vigorous little Bohemia in which idiosyncratic values of spirit could be preserved and directly expressed. Its members were determined to paint only what they themselves felt deeply, and resisted the government's attempt to revive by edict Italy's cultural supremacy. Their decision might seem inevitable to artists working under a democratic regime; in the Italy of 1930 it was difficult and courageous.

Two years younger than Mafai, the tubercular Scipione, who died at twenty-nine, was the founder of the "Roman School" and its leading figure. He might be described as a Modigliani who stayed at home, though he was certainly a lesser artist than his expatriate countryman. Like Modigliani he produced in a few years a body of work whose influence and prestige are very much alive today. And it is a curious fact that the painter from whom Scipione learned most was Modigliani's old companion in Paris, Chaim Soutine. Though he is said not to have seen a picture by Soutine until toward the end of his life, Scipione knew the Lithuanian artist's work from reproductions, and on this indirect evidence partly based his own agitated technique. His career began around 1927 and virtually ended in 1931, when illness forced him to enter a hospital. Within these four years he compressed his life work, painting still lifes (pl. 90), portraits of friends and of Cardinals, and romantic images of favorite Italian squares (pl. 91). A vivid fantasy runs through much of his art. His elegant, springy line, blotting occasionally in expressionist whorls, at times reveals the influence of Pascin, Chagall or George Grosz. He was more original as a colorist; his rich, somber, yet fervid handling of pigment is intensely personal. His early death was a major blow to contemporary Italian art.

The painting of Mario Mafai illustrates, more directly than that of Scipione, the nature of the "Roman School's" reaction away from the *Novecento*. In the time of Fascism's thunderous springtime, when rebirth and blossoming were the studio order of the day, Mafai painted withered leaves and flowers in the open sunlight (pl. 94)— "I put them there as if arranged by chance with no compositional intention whatever." In the Rome that Mussolini had decreed must be the eternal capital of the new Caesars, he portrayed scenes of demolition, of old buildings slithering to the ground to make way for triumphal boulevards. Like Scipione, he was more interested in prostitutes than in symbolic figures of Italian womanhood, and even his more innocent nudes are presented in a mood of private nostalgia rather than of allegorical proclamation. His art is less esteemed in Italy than that of Scipione, quite possibly because in recent years his romanticism has become diffused and often weak. Yet if he was less inventive than his colleague, during the short existence of the "Roman School," he was perhaps a fresher painter. Indeed, the younger generation in Italy has produced few images which can compare in sheer sensibility to the best of Mafai's still lifes of 1930-35.

Today the influence of the "Roman School" is felt in various directions. Scipione's revitalization of Soutine's expressionism is continued both by GIOVANNI STRADONE and TOTI SCIALOJA (pls. 95 and 96), while Mafai's early *Landscape with Train* (pl. 92) foretells the neo-romanticism of RENZO VESPIGNANI (pl. 101). It is the last-named artist who has become the leader of the extremely young group of Roman artists which includes MARCELLO MUCCINI and GRAZIELLA URBINATI. All of them still in their early twenties, these three painters have turned their backs on the wave of abstraction which now so thoroughly dominates the current Italian art scene, and have launched a movement which compares in emphasis on human sentiment with the Parisian neo-romantic revolt of 1926. The astonishingly fluent calligraphy of Vespignani (pl. 100) proposes a delicate yet piercing commentary on post-war Italy, with its heritage of destruction and melancholy. While Guttuso and other artists of the *Fronte nuovo delle arti* are motivated by aggressive hope, Vespignani is essentially a *poète maudit*. His painting, however, is thus far less distinguished than his graphic art, whereas Muccini, whose drawing is gradually outgrowing a dependence on Toulouse-Lautrec, is already a painter of considerable distinction (pl. 98). Together the two artists, and with them the girl Graziella, have survived their precocity and are today among the most interesting figures of the newest generation.

The Fantasts

During the recent war, the Argentine-born member of the newer School of Paris, Leonor Fini, lived and worked in Italy. A forceful personality, she almost immediately had a decided influence on Italian artists with a predilection for fantasy, for the chimerical imagery produced at intervals during the sixteenth, seventeenth and eighteenth centuries. Leonor Fini had herself come to maturity in the atmosphere of Parisian surrealism and neo-romanticism. She arrived in Italy an accomplished painter and became the muse for a revival of fantasy, particularly in Rome. Perhaps her only direct disciple was STANISLAO LEPRI (pl. 104), but her presence in Italy undoubtedly helped popularize the fanciful trend of the solitary GIUSEPPE VIVIANI (pl. 103) and of FABRIZIO CLERICI (pl. 102). Yet the graphic work of the latter two men is also a continuation of the native "metaphysical" school, as carried on by Alberto Savinio. And the *scuola metafisica* in its original, powerful stages has been revived recently by the talented young Milanese artist, SALVATORE FIUME, whose *Island of Statues* (pl. 105) pays tribute to de Chirico's *Disquieting Muses* of 1916.

The Younger Abstractionists; the Fronte nuovo delle arti

As we have seen in discussing the "Roman School" of 1930, a reaction against the nationalistic traditionalism of the *Novecento* had begun soon after the latter movement's first exhibition of 1926. The reaction, however, had of necessity been nourished locally for the most part; its supplementary diet usually consisted of reproductions of foreign art rather than of the art itself. Few younger Italian painters could afford to travel to Paris; few contemporary foreign works made their way to Italy. Indeed, to appreciate the isolation of Italian painting during the Fascist regime, we need only remember that the first comprehensive exhibition in Italy of the French impressionists was held at the Venice Biennial Exposition of 1948.

With the end of the recent war the situation changed abruptly. Not only did the more successful younger artists like Birolli and Guttuso visit Paris, but the full tide of advanced European art poured into Italy (at the Biennial Exposition of 1948, for example, were assembled representative groups of works by Braque, Rouault, Chagall, Henry Moore, Kokoschka, Picasso and others).

Picasso especially, who had seemed a distant thunder, became a tremendous force among painters of the newer generation who were eager to join the international mainstream of contemporary art. Since 1945, these painters have made a valiant attempt to regain the progressive momentum which had died out in their country after the collapse of Futurism and the *scuola metafisica*, though it had been preserved abroad by an occasional exile like the fine abstractionist, Alberto Magnelli, whose works unfortunately were not available for the present exhibition. In a sense the Italians' long segregation has become a current asset; unlike the younger French, for whom the revolution of their elders is a rather oppressive *fait accompli*, they work with fresh eagerness—to catch up and to move ahead.

At the very outset of the war, the painter Renato Birolli had gathered around him at Milan a few of his contemporaries who were anxious to go beyond the "Roman School's" insurrection against the *Novecento*. Known as the *Corrente*, the movement was dispersed by the war, but in 1946, again on Birolli's initiative, the *Nuova secessione artistica italiana* was formed and issued a manifesto signed by eleven artists—Birolli, Cassinari, Corpora, Guttuso, Leoncillo, Morlotti, Pizzinato, Santomaso, Turcato, Vedova and Viani. The following year the group's name was changed to the *Fronte nuovo delle arti*, and Cassinari resigned, to be replaced by the sculptors, Fazzini and Franchina. But its ideals remained the same. As the 1946 manifesto had declared, these artists wished "to give their observations and their separate creations in the world of the imagination a basis of moral necessity and to bring them together as expressions of life." They added: "Art is not the conventional face of history; it is history itself, which does not exist apart from man."

From these words, despite a deliberate lack of dogmatic precision, it is clear that the artists of the *Fronte* are intent on bringing their art to grips with contemporary reality, specifically with the humanitarian reality in which the majority of them are vitally interested as men of left-wing political convictions. But the art in which they believe is that which has evolved from cubism and its later abstract ramifications and, to a lesser degree, from expressionism. No one of them has shown any inclination whatever to return to traditional realism of technique; it is such a work as Picasso's *Guernica* which is their ideal, and not academic propaganda art in the Soviet Union.

The most forceful figure in the *Fronte* is RENATO GUTTUSO, by now very likely the best known younger painter in Europe. Since 1942 Guttuso has abandoned the expressionism of his *Battle with Wounded Horses* (pl. 106), and has taken as point of departure Picasso's paintings of the past fifteen years. He has, however, recurrently retained a clear reference to contemporary actuality, as in his painting (color plate opposite) of the dreaded Sicilian *Maffia* shooting down innocent peasants. Today he uses still life primarily as a discipline (pl. 107), as a means of perfecting those lusty elisions of contour and tone on which his art is now based; his preferred subject is the dignity of the people, preserved in the face of oppression and poverty (pl. 108). The impact of Picasso's discoveries may still be felt in Guttuso's paintings, but he has nevertheless achieved a memorable, individual style, particularly in his bold, emphatically Italian use of color. His paintings, as Ingeborg Eichmann has properly remarked, almost have "the clarity of woodcuts," of those devout images of the fifteenth century in which a quite different faith was proclaimed with all the crude strength of which the artist was capable.

It was never the intention of the *Fronte* to impose a group style on its members, and the two Venetian artists, ARMANDO PIZZINATO and GIUSEPPE SANTOMASO, are very different from each other and from Guttuso. The more daring of the two is Pizzinato (pl. 113), whose primary interest is forms in motion, as it had been for the Futurists nearly forty years before. But whereas the Futurists had often made use of neo-impressionism's divided tones (pl. 22), Pizzinato's art is

GUTTUSO: *The Maffia*, 1948. Oil on canvas, 27⅞ x 35½". Collection the Museum of Modern Art, New York.

expressed through broad, lurid contrasts of color, related to the later painting of Picasso. He is the most vigorous member of the *Fronte* except Guttuso. Santomaso, on the other hand, is essentially a tonal painter in the Venetian tradition (pl. 112). His soft, handsome colors and beguiling serenity bring him closer to Braque and La Fresnaye than to Picasso. At Milan, however, the seceding member of the *Fronte*, BRUNO CASSINARI, has turned his back on the great Parisian semi-abstractions of the past thirty years, and has developed in solitude a rich expressionist figure style (pl. 97); his closest sympathy is for the art of Modigliani. And at Rome two painters, CORRADO CAGLI and AFRO, though not enrolled in the *Fronte*, are nevertheless related in general tendency to Guttuso, Pizzinato and Santomaso. The art of Afro, even if non-representational, is notable for its warm elegance and romantic mood, while Cagli (pl. 109) has added to abstraction an element of enigmatic mystery by reviving in a personal manner the strong linear perspective and dramatic shadows of de Chirico's "metaphysical" period.

Recent Sculpture

Whereas late nineteenth-century Italy had produced in Medardo Rosso a sculptor of international importance and influence, the finest Italian sculpture of the early twentieth century was created by the painters, Boccioni (pls. 12 and 13) and Modigliani (pls. 47 and 48). Over the past twenty years, however, sculptural preeminence has reverted to the profession, and the outstanding sculptors of contemporary Italy are the so-called "Three M's"—ARTURO MARTINI, who died in 1947, MARINO MARINI and GIACOMO MANZÙ.

Martini was born at Treviso and trained at Munich under Adolf Hildebrand. His erratic but sometimes brilliant career began in the era of the *scuola metafisica*. To that period belongs his *Portrait of Chekhov* (pl. 115), with its extreme stylization and sleek finish. During his later career Martini turned at intervals to the appealing naturalism exemplified by *The Fisherman's Wife* (pl. 114). Yet a rude, powerful expressionism was never long absent from his work (pl. 116), nor was a sense of archaic grandeur which drew equally on primitive and Mannerist sources. Often interested in extreme muscular tensions, he produced a distraught figure style, feverish in its eclecticism, tragic in spirit, but marked at its best by a convincing vehemence.

The art of Marino Marini, contrarily, is notable for its steady growth in eloquence and authority. An immensely cultivated man, who has lived much abroad and traveled widely, Marini is today one of the few major figures of his generation in European sculpture. He has reacted completely away from the burnished surfaces of Brancusi's works in brass and marble, and has given his bronzes a painted patina, white and gilt, carefully manipulated to provide a strong textural interest (pl. 120). Moreover, among his more remarkable accomplishments is the expressive skill through which his basic forms are incised to establish character, as in the horseman's head of the large *Horse and Rider* (pl. 119). Indeed his sensitivity to the particularities of character has made him one of the finest portraitists of our time (pl. 121), a master of those notched accents whereby the set of a mouth or the glance of an eye is fixed unchangeably—and becomes at the same time a telling hieroglyphic motif, as in the portraits by the Roman sculptors. Yet Marini is above all an inventor of broad-scale, contemporary forms. In recent years, inspired by the memory of peasants fleeing the bombings, remembering, too, the early Ming horses, he has created a series of horsemen whose unforgettable humanism is conveyed by intensely felt values of plastic weight, thrust and proportion. His presence in Italy today is an extraordinary asset in the resurgence of creative impetus among the younger men.

Marini's slightly younger contemporary, Giacomo Manzù, is a different kind of sculptor altogether—warm, tender, romantic, belonging essentially to older sculptural traditions. His *Portrait of a Lady* (pl. 125), is a moving and gracious work of art, achieving an atmospheric magnetism through its delicacy of line and surface. But Manzù has a more violent side. During the recent war he courageously executed a fine series of bas-reliefs on the Crucifixion, in one of which the mocking soldier is a helmeted German infantryman (pl. 124). Manzù is a deeply religious man, and throughout his career has done bronze figures of Cardinals (pl. 123). It seems a pity that the Church, which has censured his art, has not made more use of his great talents.

Working at Rome, the two even younger sculptors, PERICLE FAZZINI and EMILIO GRECO, have followed divergent paths. Fazzini's deliberate Mannerism is particularly impressive in the *Seated Woman* (pl. 127), which fulfills the promise already so clear in his more direct *Portrait of Ungaretti* (pl. 126). Greco, for his part, has evolved a bland, neo-classical style which is not, however, concerned with idealization so much as with acute characterization; the lively realism of his *Singer* (pl. 130) is abetted rather than muffled by his solemn contours. At the opposite technical extreme is LUCIO FONTANA, once an abstract Constructivist, whose fluid handling of ceramic is in the expressionist vein (pl. 131). With MASCHERINI's bold, forceful *Cock* (pl. 122), modern Italian sculpture again rejoins the Mannerist road. With VIANI's extremely fine *Nude* (pl. 133), it moves forward drastically, to join the biomorphic "concretions" of Jean Arp and other leaders of the Parisian vanguard.

1. BOCCIONI: *Street Pavers*, 1910? Oil on canvas, 39⅜ x 39⅜". Collection Romeo Toninelli, Milan.

Below: 2. BOCCIONI: Study for *The City Rises*, 1910. Crayon and chalk, 22½ x 33½". Collection Vico Baer, New York.

Opposite above: 6. BOCCIONI: *States of Mind*, III: *Those Who Stay*, 1911. Oil on canvas, 27⅛ x 38⅜″. Collection Donna Benedetta Marinetti, Rome. Number I, *The Farewells*, is reproduced in color.

Opposite below: 7. BOCCIONI: *States of Mind*, II: *Those Who Go*, 1911. Oil on canvas, 27⅛ x 37⅜″. Collection Donna Benedetta Marinetti, Rome.

I, *The Farewells.*

III, *Those Who Stay.*

II, *Those Who Go.*

3-5. BOCCIONI: Studies for *States of Mind*, I, II and III (*The Farewells, Those Who Go, Those Who Stay*), 1911. Pencil, 23 x 34″. Collection the Museum of Modern Art, New York. Gift of Vico Baer.

Opposite: 10. BOCCIONI: *Materia*, 1912. Oil on canvas, 90⅜ x 49¼". Collection Romeo Toninelli, Milan.

8. BOCCIONI: *Elasticity*, 1912. Oil on canvas, 39⅜ x 39⅜". Collection Donna Benedetta Marinetti, Rome.

9. BOCCIONI: Study for *Materia*, 1912. Pencil, 17⅞ x 23⅞". A. Bertarelli Collection, Castello Sforzesco, Milan.

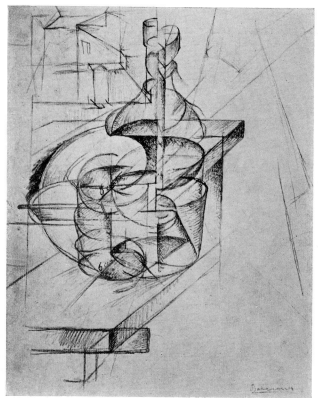

Opposite: 13. Boccioni: *Unique Forms of Continuity in Space*, 1913. Bronze, 43½″ high. Collection the Museum of Modern Art, New York. Acquired through the Lillie P. Bliss Bequest.

11. Boccioni: *Analysis of a Bottle*, 1912-13. Pencil, 13⅛ x 9⁷⁄₁₆″. The A. Bertarelli Collection, Castello Sforzesco, Milan.

Below: 12. Boccioni: *Development of a Bottle in Space*, 1912. Bronze, 15″ high. Collection the Museum of Modern Art, New York. Aristide Maillol Fund.

14. BOCCIONI: *Woman at a Table: Interpenetration of Lights and Planes*, 1914? Oil on canvas, 33⅞ x 33⅞". Collection the Galleria d'Arte Moderna, Milan.

15. BOCCIONI: *Charge of Lancers*, 1915. Tempera and collage on cardboard, 20 x 13". Collection Adriano Pallini, Milan.

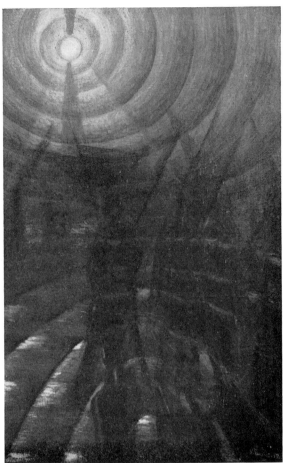

17. RUSSOLO: *The Fog*, 1912. Oil on canvas. Collection Donna Margherita Sarfatti, Rome.

16. BOCCIONI: *Muscular Dynamism*, 1913. Charcoal, 23⅛ x 22½". Collection Donna Benedetta Marinetti, Rome.

Above: 18. CARRÀ: *Funeral of the Anarchist Galli,* 1911? Oil on canvas, 78¼ x 102″. Collection the Museum of Modern Art, New York. Acquired through the Lillie P. Bliss Bequest.

19. CARRÀ: *The Tram,* 1911? Oil on canvas, 20½ x 26¼″. Collection Eugenio Ventura, Florence.

Above: 20. SEVERINI: *Boulevard*,
1910-11. Oil on canvas, 25½ x 36¼".
Collection Fred H. Mayor, London.

21. SEVERINI: *The Train in the City*,
1913? Charcoal, 19⅝ x 25⅝". The
Estate of Alfred Stieglitz, New York.

22. SEVERINI: *Dynamic Hieroglyphic of The Bal Tabarin*, 1912. Oil on canvas with sequins, 63⅝ x 61½". Collection the Museum of Modern Art, New York.

23. SEVERINI: *Armored Train*, 1915. Oil on canvas, 46 x 34½". Collection Mr. and Mrs. Charles J. Liebman, New York.

24. SEVERINI: *Dancer-Helix-Sea*, 1915. Oil on canvas, 30⅝ x 29⅝". The Estate of Alfred Stieglitz, New York.

Above: 25. BALLA: *Leash in Motion,* 1912.
Oil on canvas, 35¾ x 43⅜″. Collection
A. Conger Goodyear, New York.

26. BALLA: *Girl × Balcony,* 1912. Oil on
canvas, 48⅞ x 48⅞″. Owned by the artist.

Above: 27. BALLA: *Swifts: Paths of Movement + Dynamic Sequences,* 1913. Oil on canvas, 38⅛ x 47⅜″. Collection the Museum of Modern Art, New York.

28. BALLA: Study for *Swifts,* 1913. Watercolor, 9¼ x 14⅛″. Private collection, New York.

Above: 29. BALLA: *Speeding Automobile*, 1912. Oil on wood, 21⅛ x 27⅛". Collection the Museum of Modern Art, New York.

30. SOFFICI: *Still Life*, 1914. Oil and collage on canvas, 18⅛ x 15". Collection Cesare Tosi, Milan.

31. DE CHIRICO: *Nostalgia of the Infinite*, 1913-14? Oil on canvas, 53¼ x 25½". Collection the Museum of Modern Art, New York.

32. De Chirico: *Melancholy and Mystery of a Street*, 1914. Oil on canvas, 34¼ x 28⅛″. Private collection.

33. DE CHIRICO: *Seer*, 1915. Oil on canvas, 35¼ x 27⅜″. Private collection.

34. DE CHIRICO: *Metaphysical Interior with Large Building*, 1916. Oil on canvas, 37¾ x 28¹⁵⁄₁₆″. Collection Carlo Frua de Angeli, Milan.

35. De Chirico: *Sacred Fish*, 1917 (or 1915?). Oil on canvas, 29⁹⁄₁₆ x 24¼″. Collection Carlo Frua de Angeli, Milan.

Opposite: 36. De Chirico: *Grand Metaphysician*, 1917. Oil on canvas, 40½ x 27½″. Collection Philip L. Goodwin, New York.

37. CARRÀ: *Drunken Gentleman*, 1916. Oil on canvas, 23⅝ x 17½″. Collection Carlo
Frua de Angeli, Milan.

Opposite above: 38. CARRÀ: *The Cavalier of the West*, 1917. Oil on canvas,
21 x 23″. Collection Adriano Pallini, Milan.

Opposite below: 39. CARRÀ: *Still Life with Triangle*, 1917. Oil on canvas,
17⅜ x 23⅞″. Collection Riccardo Jucker, Milan.

41. CARRÀ: *The Engineer's Mistress*, 1921. Oil on canvas, 21⅝ x 15¾″. The Gianni Mattioli Foundation, Milan. Feroldi Collection.

Opposite: 40. CARRÀ: *Hermaphroditic Idol*, 1917. Oil on canvas, 25⅝ x 16⁹⁄₁₆″. Collection Carlo Frua de Angeli, Milan.

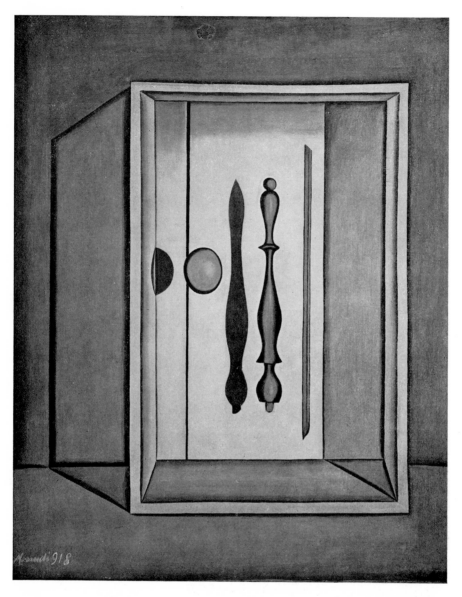

42. MORANDI: *Still Life with Box and Ninepin*, 1918. Oil on canvas, 25⅝ x 21¼″. Collection
Riccardo Jucker, Milan.

Opposite above: 43. MORANDI: *Objects*, 1919. Oil on canvas, 20⅜ x 21¾″.
Collection Dr. Roberto Longhi, Florence.

Opposite below: 44. MORANDI: *Mannequin on a Round Table*, 1918. Oil on canvas,
19¼ x 23¼″. Collection Riccardo Jucker, Milan.

45. MODIGLIANI: *Seated Nude*, 1918. Oil on canvas, 32½ x 26⅜". Collection Leigh B. Block, Chicago.

46. MODIGLIANI: *The Servant*, 1919. Oil on canvas, 60 x 24″.
Collection the Albright Art Gallery, Buffalo. Room of Contemporary Art.

MODIGLIANI:
47. *Caryatid*, c.1919. Stone, 36¼" high. The Buchholz Gallery.
48. *Head*, c.1915? Stone, 22¼" high. Museum of Modern Art.

49. MODIGLIANI: *A Portrait of a Young Woman.* Pencil, 11⅛ x 7⅞".
The Fogg Museum of Art, Harvard University, Cambridge, Mass.

Right: 50. MODIGLIANI: *Man with a Hat,* 1920. Pencil, 19¼ x 12".
Collection the Museum of Modern Art, New York.

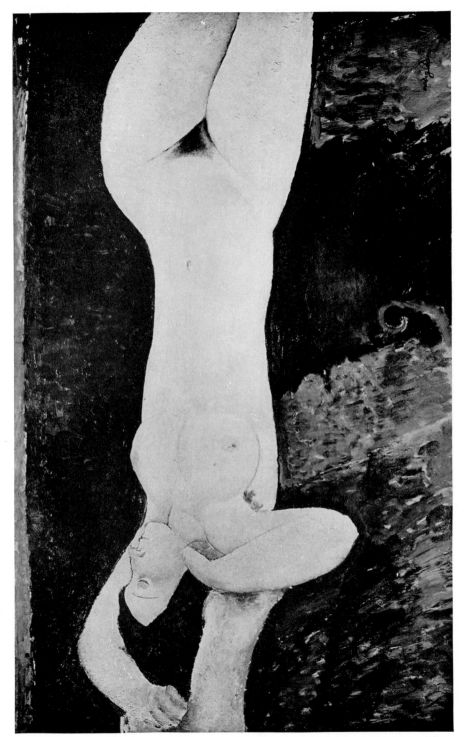

51. MODIGLIANI: *Reclining Nude*. 1918? Oil on canvas, 28¾ x 45¾". Collection Josef von Sternberg, Weehawken, New Jersey.

53. MODIGLIANI: *Bride and Groom*, 1915-16. Oil on canvas, 21¾ x 18¼". Collection the Museum of Modern Art, New York. Gift of Frederic Clay Bartlett.

Left: 52. MODIGLIANI: *Jacques Lipchitz and His Wife.* Oil on canvas, 31½ x 21". The Art Institute of Chicago. Helen Birch Bartlett Memorial Collection.

54. De Chirico: *The Departure of the Knight Errant*, 1923. Oil on canvas, 38 x 50". Collection Adriano Pallini, Milan.

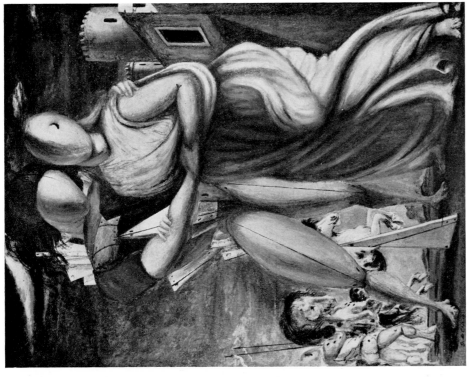

56. DE CHIRICO: *Hector and Andromache*, 1924. Oil and tempera on canvas, 28⅝ x 39⅛". Collection Romeo Toninelli, Milan.

55. DE CHIRICO: *Roman Villa*, 1922. Tempera, 40 x 30". Collection G. Bruno Pagliai, Mexico City.

58. MORANDI: *Still Life with Bottles and Fruit Dish*, 1916. Oil on canvas, 23⅝ x 21¼". The Gianni Mattioli Foundation, Milan. Feroldi Collection.

Opposite: 57. MORANDI: *Still Life*, 1916. Oil on canvas, 32½ x 22⅝". Collection the Museum of Modern Art, New York.

59. MORANDI: *Flowers*, 1918. Oil on canvas,
32⅟₁₆ x 26⅜″. Private collection, Milan.

60. MORANDI: *Landscape*, 1933. Etching, 8⅟₁₆ x 11¹³⁄₁₆″. Collection the
Museum of Modern Art, New York.

61. MORANDI: *Landscape*. Oil on canvas. Collection Pietro Rollino, Rome.

Below: 62: MORANDI: *Still Life*, 1937. Oil on canvas, 17¾ x 23¼". Collection Viscount Dr. Franco Marmont, Milan.

63. CARRÀ: *Morning at the Seaside*, 1928. Oil on canvas, 25¼ x 21¼″. The Gianni Mattioli Foundation, Milan. Feroldi Collection.

64. TOSI: *San Giorgio Maggiore*, 1945. Oil on canvas, 19¾ x 23⅝″. Owned by the artist.

65. TOSI: *Still Life*, 1947. Oil on canvas, 19¾ x 15³⁄₁₆″. Owned by the artist.

Opposite: 67. CASORATI: *City Dwellers*, 1930. Oil on canvas, 59½ x 33″. Collection the Museum of Fine Arts, Boston.

66. CASORATI: *Eggs on a Table*, 1920. Oil on wood, 20½ x 24⁷⁄₁₆″. Collection Sra. Daphne Maugham Casorati, Turin.

68. SIRONI: *Urban Landscape*, 1929. Oil on canvas, 27⅝ x 31⅛″. The Galleria del Cavallino, Venice.

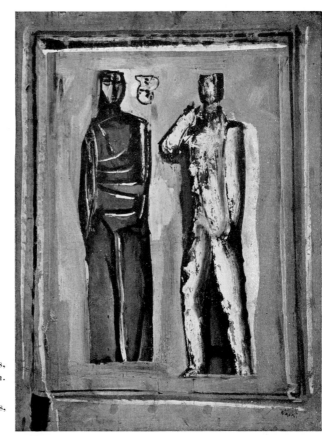

69. SIRONI: *Light Spaces*, 1941. Tempera on canvas, 31⅞ x 24⅜". Collection Carlo Frua de Angeli, Milan.

Below: 70. SIRONI: *The Flagellation*, 1948. Oil on canvas, 15¾ x 23⅝". Collection Cesare Tosi, Milan.

71. CAMPIGLI: *Happy Isle*, 1928. Oil on canvas, 39⅜ x 31⅞″. Collection Carlo Frua de Angeli, Milan.

Opposite above: 72. CAMPIGLI: *The Mariners' Wives*, 1932. Oil on canvas, 28¾ x 34⅝″. Collection Viscount Dr. Franco Marmont, Milan.

Opposite below: 73. CAMPIGLI: *The Hairdressers*, 1936. Oil on canvas, 28⅜ x 39⅜″. The Galleria del Cavallino, Venice.

74. CAMPIGLI: *The Staircase*, 1941.
Oil on canvas, 35⁷⁄₁₆ x 19¾". Collection Raffaele Carrieri, Milan.

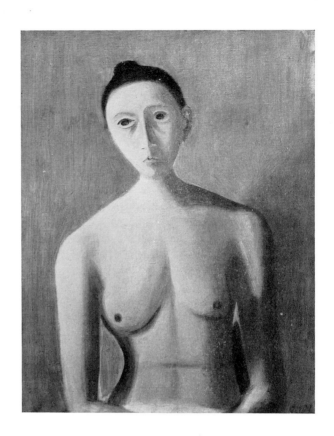

Above: 75. GUIDI: *Nude,* 1945. Oil on canvas. Owned by the artist.

76. GUIDI: *Figures in Space,* 1947. Oil on canvas. Owned by the artist.

79. DE PISIS: *The Door of My Studio*, 1935. Oil, 39¼ x 31½". Collection Dr. Lionello Venturi, Rome.

Opposite above: 77. DE PISIS: *Still Life with Funnel and Shopping Bag*, 1925.
Oil, 20⅛ x 27³⁄₁₆". Collection Viscount Dr. Franco Marmont, Milan.

Opposite below: 78. DE PISIS: *Poultry Yard*, 1928. Oil on wood, 16½ x 23".
Collection Dr. Giuseppe Vismara, Milan.

Above: 80. BORRA: *Concert for Two Flutes,*
1947. Oil on canvas, 41⅜ x 49¼". Owned
by the artist.

81. BORRA: *The Refugees,* 1948. Oil on canvas, 15¾ x 19⅞". Owned by the artist.

82. DONGHI: *The Hunter*, 1940. Oil on canvas, 42 x 31½". Collection Giovanni Merlo, Rome.

83. ROSAI: *Billiard Players*, 1921. Oil on canvas, 10¼ x 11¼″. Collection A. Gonnelli, Florence.

Below: 84. ROSAI: *Still Life with Powder Box*, 1919. Oil on canvas, 11⅞ x 15¾″. Collection Dr. Camillo Poli, Milan.

85. ROSAI: *My Father*, 1920. Oil on canvas, 12¼ x 10¼″. The Gianni Mattioli Foundation, Milan. Feroldi Collection.

Below: 86. ROSAI: *Composition with a Priest*, 1920. Oil on canvas, 15¾ x 19¾″. The Galleria del Cavallino, Venice.

87. BARTOLINI: *Anna's Dream*, 1941. Etching, 13³⁄₁₆ x 11⅛". Collection the Museum of Modern Art, New York.

88. BARTOLINI: *High Heels*, 1946. Etching, 5¾ x 6¼". Collection the Museum of Modern Art, New York.

89. PIRANDELLO: *Bathers*. Oil on wood. Collection Dr. Augusto Caraceni, Rome.

90. SCIPIONE: *Still Life with Hat, Stick and Comb*, 1929. Oil on canvas, 23⅝ x 27⅝". The Galleria del Cavallino, Venice.

91. Scipione: *Piazza Navona*, 1930. Oil on wood, 31⁵⁄₁₆ x 31¾". Collection Princess Margherita Caetani di Bassiano, Rome.

92. MAFAI: *Landscape with Train*, 1928. Oil on wood, 11⅜ x 15⅜″. Collection Ferrucio Asta, Milan.

93. MAFAI: *Nude*, 1933. Oil. Collection the Galleria Nazionale d'Arte Moderna, Rome.

94. MAFAI: *Dry Leaves and Carnations*, 1934. Oil on canvas, 27⅝ x 21¼″. Collection Dr. Giulio Laudisa, Rome.

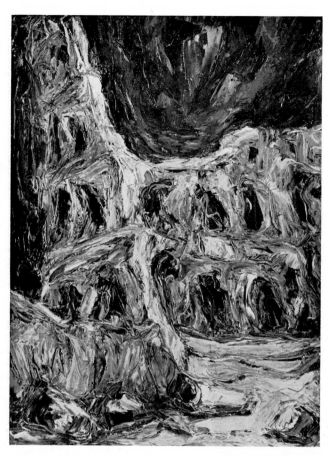

95. STRADONE: *The Colosseum*, 1945. Oil on canvas, 25⅝ x 19¾″. Collection Dr. Giulio Laudisa, Rome.

96. SCIALOJA: *Factories on the Tiber*, 1946. Oil on canvas, 23⅝ x 27⅝″. Owned by the artist.

97. CASSINARI: *The Mother*, 1948. Oil on canvas, 47½ x 29¾". Collection the Museum of Modern Art, New York.

98. MUCCINI: *Bull*, 1948. Duco on plywood, 13 x 28¼″. Collection the Museum of Modern Art, New York.

99. MUCCINI: *Tragic Moment*, 1949. Charcoal, 17½ x 26″. Collection Nelson A. Rockefeller, New York.

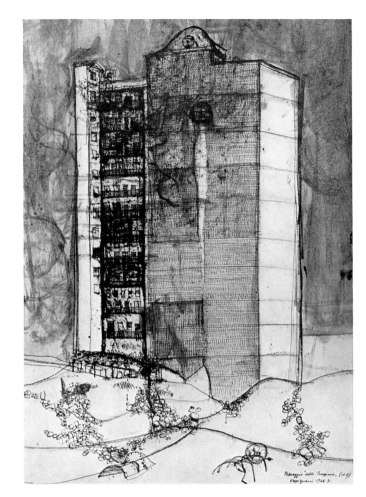

100. VESPIGNANI: *Ruined Building*, 1946. Pen and ink wash, 14¾ x 10¾″. Collection the Museum of Modern Art, New York.

Below: 101. VESPIGNANI: *The Wall*, 1947. Pen and ink wash, 7½ x 18⅜″. Collection the Museum of Modern Art, New York.

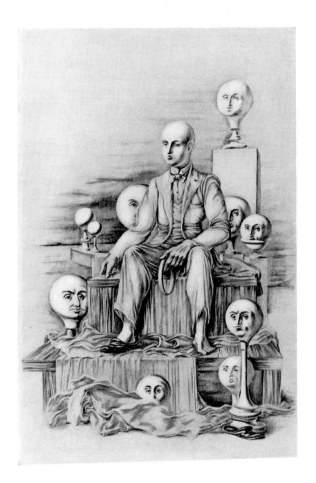

Opposite above: 104. LEPRI: *Luncheon in the Tower,* 1946. Gouache, 15¾ x 19½″. The Hugo Gallery, New York.

Opposite below: 105. FIUME: *Island of Statues,* 1948. Oil on canvas, 28 x 36¼″. Collection the Museum of Modern Art, New York.

102. CLERICI: *Spherical Obsession.* 1944. Pencil. Collection Peter Lindamood, New York.

103. VIVIANI: *The Leg,* 1939. Etching, 7¾ x 11⅞″. Collection the Museum of Modern Art, New York.

108. GUTTUSO: *Sleeping Carter*, 1946. Oil on canvas, 19¾ x 23⅝″. Collection Dino Zanardo, Rome.

Opposite above: 106. GUTTUSO: *Battle with Wounded Horses*, 1942. Oil on canvas, 18½ x 22⅞″. Collection the Galleria Nazionale d'Arte Moderna, Rome.

Opposite below: 107. GUTTUSO: *Artichoke and Apple*, 1946. Oil on canvas, 13¾ x 17¾″. Owned by the artist.

109. CAGLI: Study for *Spies at the Stake*, 1947. Oil on canvas, 41 x 27″. Private collection.

110, AFRO: *Trophy*, 1948. Oil on canvas, 49¼ x
23⅝″. The Galleria dell' Obelisco, Rome.

111. SANTOMASO: *Still Life with Chicken*, 1948. Oil on canvas, 23⅝ x 29½″. Owned by the artist.

Below: 112. SANTOMASO: *Fisherman*, 1948. Oil on canvas, 23⅝ x 35½″. Owned by the artist.

113. PIZZINATO: *Defenders of the Factory*, 1948. Oil on board, 26⅜ x 38⅝″. Collection the Galleria Internazionale d'Arte Moderna, Venice.

114. MARTINI: *The Fisherman's Wife*. Terra cotta. Collection
Count Contini Bonacossi, Florence.

Below: 115. MARTINI: *Portrait of Chekhov*, 1919. Terra cotta,
17¾″ high. Collection Adriano Pallini, Milan.

116. MARTINI: *Daedalus and Icarus*, 1934-35. Bronze, 24″ high. Collection Mrs. Brigida Martini, Rome.

Opposite: 118. MARINI: *Nude*, 1943.
Bronze, 52½″ high. The Buchholz
Gallery, New York.

117. MARINI. *Prizefighter*, 1935.
Bronze, 26½″ high. Collection Dr.
W. R. Valentiner, Los Angeles.

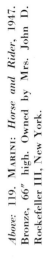

Above: 119. MARINI: *Horse and Rider*, 1947. Bronze, 66" high. Owned by Mrs. John D. Rockefeller III, New York.

120. MARINI: *Horse and Rider*, 1948. Bronze, 38¼" high. Collection the Museum of Modern Art, New York.

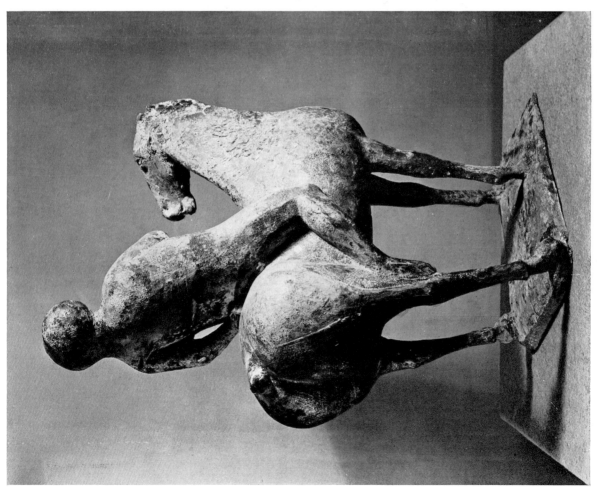

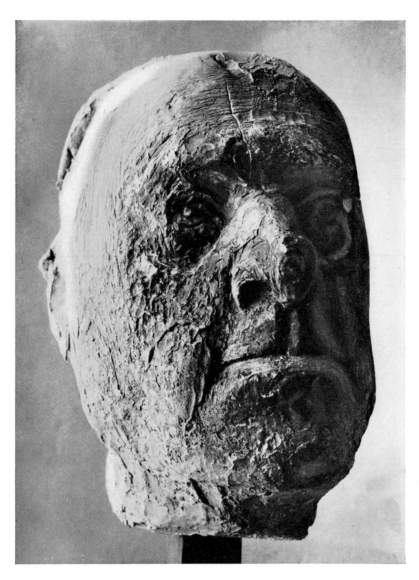

121. MARINI: *Portrait of Carlo Carrà*, 1947. Bronze, 9⅛" high. Owned by the artist.

122. MASCHERINI: *Cock*, 1948. Bronze, 19¾". Owned by the artist.

Above: 123. MANZÙ: *Cardinal*, 1938. Bronze, 20½" high. Collection the Galleria Nazionale d'Arte Moderna, Rome.

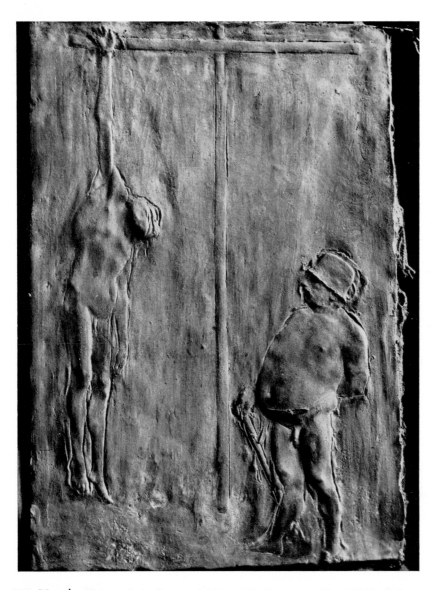

124. MANZÙ: *Christ and the German Soldier*, 1942. Bronze, 11¾ x 15¾". Collection Dr. Riccardo Gualino, Rome.

Opposite: 125. MANZÙ: *Portrait of a Lady*, 1946. Bronze, 68⅞" high. Collection Sra. Alice Lampugnani, Milan.

126. FAZZINI: *Portrait of Ungaretti*, 1936. Wood, 23¼″ high. Collection the Galleria Nazionale d'Arte Moderna, Rome.

Above: 127. FAZZINI: *Seated Woman*, 1947. Bronze, 37⅜″ high. Owned by the artist.

128. FAZZINI: *Woman Holding Her Foot, No. 1*, 1943. Bronze, 5¹⁵⁄₁₆″ high. Owned by the artist.

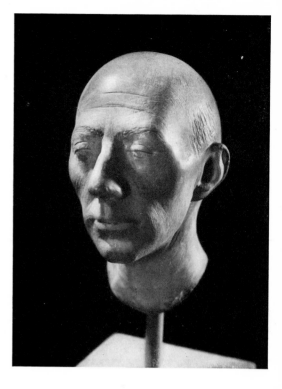

Above: 129. GRECO: *Head of a Man*, 1947. Bronze, 8¼" high. Owned by the artist.

130. GRECO: *The Singer*, 1948. Bronze, 22½" high. Owned by the artist.

Above: 131. FONTANA: *Christ*, 1947. Ceramic, $22\frac{7}{8}''$ high. Owned by the artist.

132. FONTANA: *Masker*, 1947. Ceramic, $35\frac{1}{2}''$ high. Owned by the artist.

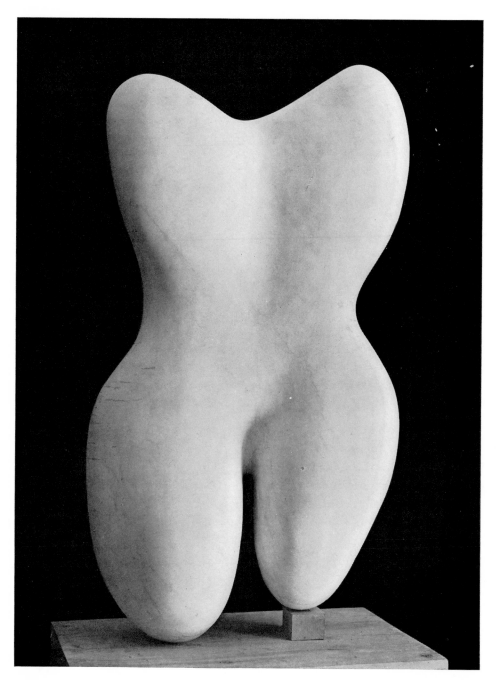

133. VIANI: *Nude*, 1945. Marble, 39¾″ high. Collection Leone Traverso, Florence.

Catalog of the Exhibition

Lenders

Ferrucio Asta, Milan; Vico Baer, New York; Giacomo Balla, Rome; Princess Margherita Caetani di Bassiano, Rome; Leigh B. Block, Chicago; Count Contini Bonacossi, Florence; Pompeo Borra, Milan; Dr. Augusto Caraceni, Rome; Carlo Carrà, Milan; Raffaele Carrieri, Milan; Mrs. Daphne Maugham Casorati, Turin; Mrs. Yvonne Casella, Rome; Mr. and Mrs. Marcellin Castaing, Paris; Antonio Donghi, Rome; Pericle Fazzini, Rome; Lucio Fontana, Milan; Carlo Frua de Angeli, Milan; A. Gonnelli, Florence; Philip L. Goodwin, New York; A. Conger Goodyear, New York; Emilio Greco, Rome; Mr. and Mrs. Jan Greenlees, Rome; Dr. Riccardo Gualino, Rome; Virgilio Guidi, Venice; Renato Guttuso, Rome; Riccardo Jucker, Milan; Mrs. Alice Lampugnani, Milan; Dr. Giulio Laudisa, Rome; Sam A. Lewisohn, New York; Mr. and Mrs. Charles J. Liebman, New York; Peter Lindamood, New York; Prof. Roberto Longhi, Florence; Giacomo Manzù, Milan; Donna Benedetta Marinetti, Rome; Marino Marini, Milan; Viscount Dr. Franco Marmont, Milan; Mrs. Brigida Martini, Rome; Marcello Mascherini, Trieste; Fred H. Mayor, London; Giovanni Merlo, Rome; G. Bruno Pagliai, Mexico City; Adriano Pallini, Milan;

Fausto Pirandello, Rome; Armando Pizzinato, Venice; Dr. Camillo Poli, Milan; Mr. and Mrs. Laurance P. Roberts, Rome; Mrs. John D. Rockefeller III, New York; Nelson A. Rockefeller, New York; Dr. Pietro Rollino, Rome; Giuseppe Santomaso, Venice; Donna Margherita Sarfatti, Rome; Toti Scialoja, Rome; Josef von Sternberg, Weehawken, N. J.; Romeo Toninelli, Milan; Arturo Tosi, Milan; Cesare Tosi, Milan; Leone Traverso, Florence; Antonio Usuelli, Milan; Dr. W. R. Valentiner, Los Angeles; Eugenio Ventura, Florence; Dr. Lionello Venturi, Rome; Dr. Giuseppe Vismara, Milan; Dino Zanardo, Rome; Dr. Zibordi, Milan.

Museum of Fine Arts, Boston; Albright Art Gallery, Buffalo, N. Y.; Fogg Museum of Art, Harvard University, Cambridge, Mass.; The Art Institute of Chicago; the A. Bertarelli Collection, Castello Sforzesco, Milan; Galleria d'Arte Moderna, Milan; Gianni Mattioli Foundation, Milan; the Estate of Alfred Stieglitz, New York; Galleria Nazionale d'Arte Moderna, Rome; Civici Musei Veneziani d'Arte e di Storia; Galleria Internazionale d'Arte Moderna, Venice.

Yale University Art Gallery, New Haven; Buchholz Gallery, New York; The Hugo Gallery, New York; Galleria dell' Obelisco, Rome; Galleria del Cavallino, Venice.

Catalog

A star preceding the title indicates that the work is illustrated. Unless otherwise indicated, height precedes width.

AFRO (BASALDELLA)

Born Udine, 1912. Now works in Rome, where he has recently become a leading figure among the younger artists who are seeking to evolve a romantic language from the lessons of the post-cubist Picasso.

Lis fuárpis. 1948. Tempera on canvas, 13¾ x 19¾". Lent by the Galleria dell'Obelisco, Rome.

* *Trophy.* 1948. Oil on canvas, 49¼ x 23⅝". Lent by the Galleria dell'Obelisco, Rome. *Ill. pl. 110*

GIACOMO BALLA

Born Turin, 1871. Studied in Paris. Taught Boccioni and Severini in Rome about 1904. Signed the *Manifesto of Futurist Painting*, 1910, but did not exhibit with the Futurists until 1912. Concentrated on kinetic problems 1912-14. Remained faithful to Futurist movement during 1920's. Now lives in Rome where he has long since returned to a representational style.

* *Girl × Balcony.* 1912. Oil on canvas, 48⅞ x 48⅞". Lent by the artist. *Ill. pl. 26*

Studies for *Girl × Balcony.* 1912. Lent by the artist.
  Pencil, pen and ink, 9¹⁄₁₆ x 11".
  Pen and ink, 7½ x 9⅞".

* *Leash in Motion.* 1912. Oil on canvas, 35¾ x 43⅜". Lent by A. Conger Goodyear, New York. *Ill. pl. 25*

* *Speeding Automobile.* 1912. Oil on wood, 21⅞ x 27⅛". The Museum of Modern Art, New York. *Ill. pl. 29*

* *Swifts: Paths of Movement + Dynamic Sequences.* 1913. Oil on canvas, 38⅛ x 47⅜". The Museum of Modern Art, New York. *Ill. pl. 27*

Studies for *Swifts.* 1913.
  * Watercolor, 9¼ x 14⅛". Private collection, New York. *Ill. pl. 28*
  Pencil, 7¾ x 9¹⁄₁₆". Lent by the artist.

LUIGI BARTOLINI

Born Cupramontana (Ancona), 1892. Painter, etcher and, like so many modern Italian artists, a writer and critic. Active in many Italian centers; now lives in Rome. As a painter, belongs to the expressionist tradition; widely respected as one of the finest graphic artists of the middle generation.

The Story of the Kingfisher. 1935. Etching, 9⅞ x 13". The Museum of Modern Art, New York.

* *Anna's Dream*. 1941. Etching, 13 3/16 x 11 1/8". The Museum of Modern Art, New York. *Ill. pl. 87*

* *High Heels*. 1946. Etching, 5 3/4 x 6 1/4". The Museum of Modern Art, New York. *Ill. pl. 88*

Lungotevere. 1947. Etching, 13 5/8 x 9 5/8". The Museum of Modern Art, New York.

UMBERTO BOCCIONI

Born Reggio Calabria, 1882. Studied with Balla in Rome and at the Academy of the Brera in Milan. Signed the first *Manifesto of Futurist Painting*, Milan, 1910; took part in all the leading Futurist exhibitions in Europe and America. The most active intelligence and probably the most original artist of the Futurist group. Worked both as painter and as sculptor. His sculpture is remarkably advanced in conception, *Unique Forms of Continuity in Space* ranking as one of the major sculptures of our time. Active as theorist as well as artist. His manifesto of Futurist sculpture (1912) extended the range of the medium by suggesting unconventional, often "mechanical" materials in which the sculptor might work. His *Pittura Scultura Futuriste* (1914) is the most comprehensive summary of the Futurist premise in art by one of its adherents. Wounded in the first World War. While convalescent, was killed in a riding accident, 1916.

* *Street Pavers*. 1910? Oil on canvas, 39 3/8 x 39 3/8". Lent by Romeo Toninelli, Milan. *Ill. pl. 1*

Study for *The City Rises*. 1910. Tempera on cardboard, 7 1/8 x 12 1/4". Lent by Romeo Toninelli, Milan.

* Study for *The City Rises*. 1910. Crayon and chalk, 22 1/2 x 33 1/2". Lent by Vico Baer, New York. *Ill. pl. 2*

* *States of Mind*. 1911. Oil on canvas, each 27 1/8 x 37 3/8". Lent by Donna Benedetta Marinetti, Rome.
  I, The Farewells. Color plate opp. p. 8
  II, Those Who Go. Ill. pl. 7
  III, Those Who Stay. Ill. pl. 6

* Studies for *States of Mind*. 1911. Pencil, each 23 x 34". The Museum of Modern Art, New York. Gift of Vico Baer.
  I, The Farewells. Ill. pl. 3
  II, Those Who Go. Ill. pl. 5
  III, Those Who Stay. Ill. pl. 4

The Artist's Mother. June 27, 1911. Pencil, 5 15/16 x 9 1/2". Lent by the A. Bertarelli Collection, Castello Sforzesco, Milan.

Study for the sculpture *Head+House+Light* (now destroyed). 1911. *Dynamic-Plastic Composition*. Pencil, 24 x 19 1/4". Lent by the A. Bertarelli Collection, Castello Sforzesco, Milan.

* *Materia*. 1912. Oil on canvas, 90 3/8 x 49 1/4". Lent by Romeo Toninelli, Milan. *Ill. pl. 10*

Studies for *Materia*. 1912. Pencil. Lent by the A. Bertarelli Collection, Castello Sforzesco, Milan.
  Seated Woman. 12 1/8 x 8 1/4".
  * Composition. 17 7/8 x 23 7/8. *Ill. pl. 9*

* *Elasticity*. 1912. Oil on canvas, 39 3/8 x 39 3/8". Lent by Donna Benedetta Marinetti, Rome. *Ill. pl. 8*

Study for *Elasticity*. 1912. Pencil with gouache, 17 1/4 x 17 1/4". The Museum of Modern Art, New York.

* *Development of a Bottle in Space*. 1912. Bronze, 15" high. The Museum of Modern Art, New York. Aristide Maillol Fund. *Ill. pl. 12*

* *Analysis of a Bottle*. 1912-13. Pencil, 13 1/8 x 9 7/16". Lent by the A. Bertarelli Collection, Castello Sforzesco, Milan. *Ill. pl. 11*

* *Unique Forms of Continuity in Space*. 1913. Bronze, 43 1/2" high. The Museum of Modern Art, New York. Acquired through the Lillie P. Bliss Bequest. *Ill. pl. 13*

* *Muscular Dynamism*. 1913. Charcoal, 23 1/8 x 22 1/2". Lent by Donna Benedetta Marinetti, Rome. *Ill. pl 16*

Dynamism of a Human Figure. 1913. Oil on canvas, 25 5/8 x 31 1/2". Lent by the Galleria d'Arte Moderna, Milan.

Six studies for *Dynamism of a Human Figure*. Pen and ink, each about 12 x 9". Lent by the A. Bertarelli Collection, Castello Sforzesco, Milan.

* Two studies for *Dynamic Force of the Cyclist*. 1913. Painting now in the collection of the Duchess of Permolata. Ink. Lent by the Yale University Art Gallery, New Haven. Société Anonyme Collection. *Ill. below*

* *Woman at a Table: Interpenetration of Lights and Planes*. 1914? Oil on canvas, 33 7/8 x 33 7/8". Lent by the Galleria d'Arte Moderna, Milan. *Ill. pl. 14*

* *Charge of Lancers*. 1915. Tempera and collage on cardboard, 20 x 13". Lent by Adriano Pallini, Milan. *Ill. pl. 15*

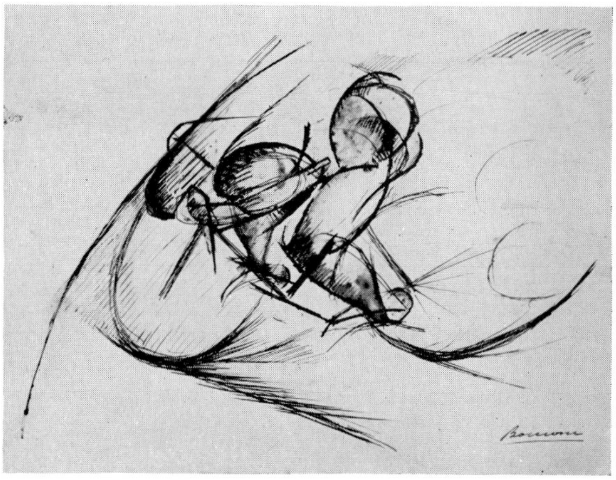

BOCCIONI: Study for the *Dynamic Force of the Cyclist* (see above).

POMPEO BORRA

Born Milan, 1898. Associated with the *Novecento* in its later stages. Worked in Paris 1936 to 1939. Imprisoned by the Nazis during the war. Turned to abstraction briefly, but has now developed an earnest and poetic style based on the fifteenth-century masters, particularly Piero della Francesca. Lives in Milan. Active as a writer on art.

* *Concert for Two Flutes*. 1947. Oil on canvas, 41⅜ x 49¼". Lent by the artist. *Ill. pl. 80*

* *The Refugees*. 1948. Oil on canvas, 15¾ x 19⅞". Lent by the artist. *Ill. pl. 81*

CORRADO CAGLI

Born Ancona, 1910. Lives in Rome and America. During the early 1930's was active as a painter and polemicist, associated with Capogrossi, Cavalli, Afro, Guttuso and other artists in a movement spiritually allied to the "Roman School" of Scipione and Mafai. Worked in a representational style, occasionally turning to allegory, but opposing *Novecento* pomposity. Served with the U. S. Army in Germany during the second World War. Has since become an abstract artist, utilizing perspective elements from de Chirico's "metaphysical" period. Numerous exhibitions in New York; designed a ballet produced in that city (1948).

Tragic Theatre. 1946. Oil on canvas, 35⁷⁄₁₆ x 23⅝". Lent by Mr. and Mrs. Laurance P. Roberts, Rome.

* Study for *Spies at the Stake*. 1947. Oil on canvas, 41 x 27". Lent anonymously. *Ill. pl. 109*

Buchenwald. 1945. Transfer drawing, 9⅞ x 12⅛". The Museum of Modern Art, New York. Purchase Fund.

MASSIMO CAMPIGLI

Born Florence, 1895. Paris, 1919 to 1939, with trips to other European centers and to New York. In youth influenced by Seurat, Picasso and Léger; has since made personal use of varied sources—Egyptan tomb painting, Pompeian and Etruscan art, medieval and early Renaissance frescoes. Now lives in Milan, and is one of the best known artists, internationally, of contemporary Italy. Represented in numerous public collections in Europe and America; many New York exhibitions. Retrospective exhibition at the Municipal Museum of Amsterdam, 1946. Awarded special gallery at the Venice Biennial Exhibition of 1948. Noted as a portraitist and for the archaic elegance of his figure paintings.

* *Happy Isle*. 1928. Oil on canvas, 39⅜ x 31⅞". Lent by Carlo Frua de Angeli, Milan. *Ill. pl. 71*

The Horseman. 1928. Oil on canvas, 14 x 15¾". Lent by Carlo Frua de Angeli, Milan.

* *The Mariners' Wives*. 1932. Oil on canvas, 28¾ x 34⅝". Lent by Viscount Dr. Franco Marmont, Milan. *Ill. pl. 72*

The Garden. 1936. Oil on canvas, 28⅜ x 36⅝". Lent by the Galleria del Cavallino, Venice.

* *The Hairdressers*. 1936. Oil on canvas, 28⅜ x 39⅜". Lent by the Galleria del Cavallino, Venice. *Ill. pl. 73*

* *The Staircase*. 1941. Oil on canvas, 35⁷⁄₁₆ x 19¾". Lent by Raffaele Carrieri, Milan. *Ill. pl. 74*

CARLO CARRÀ

Born Quargnento (Alexandria) 1881. Studied with Tallone at Academy of the Brera, Milan: influenced by Previati. One of the five original Futurist artists, 1910, and an active polemicist for that movement. In 1915 decided on a return to Giotto and other masters of the medieval and early Renaissance tradition in Italy. From 1917 to 1921 a member of the *scuola metafisica*, founded by de Chirico; had a leading part in the *scuola's* chief publication, *Valori Plastici*. Has since reverted to a more realistic subject matter and style. Included in innumerable exhibitions at home and abroad; first large one-man show at the Rome Biennial of 1924, followed by others in more recent years. The only veteran of the two principal advance-guard movements in

CARRÀ: *The Milan Galleria* (see page 128).

modern Italian art, Carrà holds a commanding position among artists of the older generation in Italy. Throughout his career he has published many books and articles on painters of the past and present; his monograph on Giotto is a standard work on that master. Lives in Milan.

FUTURIST:

* *Funeral of the Anarchist Galli.* 1911? Oil on canvas, 78¼ x 102″. The Museum of Modern Art, New York. Acquired through the Lillie P. Bliss Bequest. *Ill. pl. 18*

* *The Tram.* 1911? Oil on canvas, 20½ x 26¼″. Lent by Eugenio Ventura, Florence. *Ill. pl. 19*

* *The Milan Galleria.* 1912. Pen and ink, 6 x 4″. Lent by the artist. *Ill. p. 127*

Dancers. 1913? Conté crayon, 21⅝ x 25⅝″. Lent by the artist.

Cannon at a Gallop. 1915. Pencil, 6⅜ x 9″. Lent by the artist.

METAPHYSICAL:

* *Drunken Gentleman.* 1916. Oil on canvas, 23⅝ x 17½″. Lent by Carlo Frua de Angeli, Milan. *Ill. pl. 37*

* *The Cavalier of the West.* 1917. Oil on canvas, 21 x 23″. Lent by Adriano Pallini, Milan. *Ill. pl. 38*

* *Still Life with Triangle.* 1917. Oil on canvas, 17⅜ x 23⅞″. Lent by Riccardo Jucker, Milan. *Ill. pl. 39*

* *Hermaphroditic Idol.* 1917. Oil on canvas, 25⅝ x 16⁹⁄₁₆″. Lent by Carlo Frua de Angeli, Milan. *Ill. pl. 40*

* *The Engineer's Mistress.* 1921. Oil on canvas, 21⅝ x 15¾″. Lent by the Gianni Mattioli Foundation, Milan. Feroldi Collection. *Ill. pl. 41*

LATER:

The Pines. 1921. Oil on canvas, 28 x 22″. Lent by Mrs. Yvonne Casella, Rome.

* *Morning at the Seaside.* 1928. Oil on canvas, 25¼ x 21¼″. Lent by the Gianni Mattioli Foundation, Milan. Feroldi Collection. *Ill. pl. 63*

FELICE CASORATI

Born Novara, 1886. Educated at Padua, where he studied music and painted under the guidance of Giovanni Vianello. Naples, 1908-11. Four years of service in Italian Army during first World War. After the war moved to Turin, and has lived there ever since; now professor of painting at the Albertina Academy in that city. Primarily interested in studio figure painting. His classical restraint and compositional formality are often tempered by a romanticism of mood and atmosphere. Included in a majority of the important Italian exhibitions in recent years. Has a number of key works in collections outside Italy. Dean of the Turin painters and one of the outstanding artists of the older generation in Italy.

* *Eggs on a Table.* 1920. Oil on wood, 20½ x 24⁷⁄₁₆″. Lent by Mrs. Daphne Maugham Casorati, Turin. *Ill. pl. 66*

Room in an Inn. 1929? Oil on canvas. Lent by Donna Margherita Sarfatti, Rome.

* *City Dwellers.* 1930. Oil on canvas, 59½ x 33″. Lent by the Museum of Fine Arts, Boston. *Ill. pl. 67*

Children at Pavarolo. 1943. Oil on canvas, 33⁵⁄₁₆ x 24″. Lent by Dr. Riccardo Gualino, Rome.

Platonic Conversation. Oil on canvas. Lent by Mrs. Yvonne Casella, Rome.

Midinette. 1935. Crayon, 18⅞ x 14⅞″. Lent by Cesare Tosi, Milan.

Two lithographs from the album portfolio. 1946. 13⅞ x 10⅛″. The Museum of Modern Art, New York.
  Girl Sleeping.
  Two Women.

BRUNO CASSINARI

Born Piacenza, 1912. Now lives in Milan, where he has developed an expressionist figure style of considerable power and individuality. Influenced by Modigliani, especially in color. Associated with Birolli in the *Corrente* movement at Milan during the war. Joined Guttuso, Pizzinato, Santomaso, Viani and other artists of the younger generation in the *Fronte nuovo delle arti* (1946), but resigned in 1947, preferring to work in solitude.

* *The Mother.* 1948. Oil on canvas, 47½ x 29¾″. The Museum of Modern Art, New York. *Ill. pl. 97*

Nude. 1948. Oil on canvas, 35⅝ x 19¾″. Lent by Antonio Usuelli, Milan.

GIORGIO DE CHIRICO

Born Volo, Greece, of Italian parents, 1888. Studied the technique of art at Volo, at Athens and, after his father's death, at Munich. 1911 to 1915 in Paris, where in isolation he developed the enigmatic, troubling and deeply poetic art which led eventually to the painting of surrealism, Paris (1924).

Returned to Italy, summer, 1915. Was sent as a soldier to Ferrara. In January, 1917, at the military hospital there, met Carlo Carrà, with whom he launched the *scuola metafisica* which was later joined by Giorgio Morandi. After the war lived in Rome and Florence. Gradually turned to neo-classicism, and became absorbed in technical problems. Returned to Paris, 1925; has lived in Italy since 1940.

The most famous twentieth-century Italian artist except possibly Modigliani, de Chirico has been one of the most influential creative figures of our time. Represented in public and private collections throughout the world; innumerable one-man exhibitions. Now bitterly opposed to "modern" art of which, in youth, he was one of the most vital progenitors. Also active as a designer for the theatre.

* *Nostalgia of the Infinite.* 1913-14? (dated on painting 1911). Oil on canvas, 53¼ x 25½". The Museum of Modern Art, New York. Purchase Fund. *Ill. pl. 31*

* *Melancholy and Mystery of a Street.* 1914. Oil on canvas, 34¼ x 28⅛". Lent anonymously. *Ill. pl. 32*

* *Seer.* 1915. Oil on canvas, 35¼ x 27⅜". Lent anonymously. *Ill. pl. 33*

* *The Disquieting Muses.* 1916. Oil on canvas, 38¼ x 26". Lent by the Gianni Mattioli Foundation, Milan. Feroldi Collection. *Color frontispiece*

* *Metaphysical Interior with Large Building.* 1916. Oil on canvas, 37¾ x 28¹⁵⁄₁₆". Lent by Carlo Frua de Angeli, Milan. *Ill. pl. 34*

* *Sacred Fish.* 1917 (or 1915?). Oil on canvas, 29⁹⁄₁₆ x 24¼". Lent by Carlo Frua de Angeli, Milan. *Ill. pl. 35*

* *Grand Metaphysician.* 1917. Oil on canvas, 41¼ x 27½". Lent by Philip L. Goodwin, New York. *Ill. pl. 36*

Roman Landscape. c. 1922. Tempera. Lent by Mrs. Yvonne Casella, Rome.

* *Roman Villa.* 1922. Tempera, 40 x 30". Lent by G. Bruno Pagliai, Mexico City. *Ill. pl. 55*

* *The Departure of the Knight Errant.* 1923. Oil on canvas, 38 x 50". Lent by Adriano Pallini, Milan. *Ill. pl. 54*

* *Hector and Andromache.* 1924. Oil and tempera on canvas, 28⅝ x 39⅛". Lent by Romeo Toninelli, Milan. *Ill. pl. 56*

Day and Night. 1926. Oil on canvas, 16⅜ x 10⅞". Lent by Riccardo Jucker, Milan.

FABRIZIO CLERICI

Born Milan, 1913. Lived there until very recently, when he moved to Rome. Architect, draftsman, art historian and bibliophile. Member of the new Italian school of fantasy, with Leonor Fini as its guiding muse, which stemmed from Parisian surrealism and neo-romanticism. Author of recent book on Jan Brueghel's *Allegory of the Senses.*

* *Spherical Obsession (Man with a Ring).* 1944. Pencil, 19 x 12½". Lent by Peter Lindamood, New York. *Ill. pl. 102*

Tattered Memory. 1944. Pencil, 7⅛ x 6¼". Lent by Peter Lindamood, New York.

ANTONIO DONGHI

Born Rome, 1897. Still lives there. Studied informally at the Institute of Fine Arts, Rome. Has developed his intense realism of style in isolation from other contemporary artists and movements. His grave, painstaking art is allied in emotional simplicity to that of "primitives" like Rousseau. But it is related as well to the burnished precisions and cautious measure of certain artists of the Northern Renaissance and of classicists like Ingres.

Departure. 1932. Oil on canvas, 42⅛ x 26⅜". Lent by the artist.

Landscape. 1937. Oil on canvas, 15¾ x 19¾". Lent by the artist.

* *The Hunter.* 1940. Oil on canvas, 42 x 31½". Lent by Giovanni Merlo, Rome. *Ill. pl. 82*

PERICLE FAZZINI

Born Grottamare, 1913. At early age went to Rome, where he attended the free life classes at the Academy. Still works in Rome, and is a prominent member of the younger generation of sculptors. First national recognition at Roman Quadrennial Exposition of 1935. Principal aim is to reconcile contemporary innovation with classical discipline; recent work sometimes close to Mannerism in its elegant distortions. Joined *Fronte nuovo delle arti* at time of the group's first exhibition at the Galleria della Spiga, Milan, 1947.

* *Portrait of Ungaretti.* 1936. Wood, 23¼" high. Lent by the Galleria Nazionale d'Arte Moderna, Rome. *Ill. pl. 126*

* *Woman Holding Her Foot, No. 1.* 1943. Bronze, 5¹⁵⁄₁₆" high. Lent by the artist. *Ill. pl. 128*

Cat. 1947. Bronze, 11½" high. Lent by the artist.

* *Seated Woman.* 1947. Bronze, 37⅜" high. Lent by the artist. *Ill. pl. 127*

A group of drawings, including studies for the *Seated Woman,* lent by the artist.

SALVATORE FIUME

Young Milanese artist who has begun to paint professionally only during the past year or two. Influenced by de Chirico's "metaphysical" painting, but already showing decided imaginative gifts of his own.

* *Island of Statues.* 1948. Oil on canvas, 28 x 36¼". The Museum of Modern Art, New York. *Ill. pl. 105*

LUCIO FONTANA

Born Rosario di Santa Fé, Argentina, of an Italian father, 1899. Moved to Italy when very young and became a pupil of Wildt at the Academy of the Brera in Milan. During the mid-1930's was an abstract sculptor in the Constructivist direction; several one-man shows in Milan. Has recently abandoned the non-objective forms and machined materials of his earlier career for the expressionist figures in ceramic by which he is represented in this book.

* *Christ.* 1947. Ceramic, 22⅞" high. Lent by the artist. *Ill. pl. 131*

* *Masker.* 1947. Ceramic, 35½" high. Lent by the artist. *Ill. pl. 132*

Masker, II. 1947. Ceramic, 35½" high. Lent by the artist.

EMILIO GRECO

Born Catania, 1913. Lives in Rome. Exhibited his sculpture for the first time, 1933. His figures recall academic classicism in their restrained contours and precise surface, but are enlivened by a wry realism and decided sensitivity of execution.

* *Head of a Man.* 1947. Bronze, 8¼″ high. Lent by the artist. *Ill. pl. 129*

* *The Singer.* 1948. Bronze, 22½″ high. Lent by the artist. *Ill. pl. 130*

VIRGILIO GUIDI

Born Rome, 1892, the son of a sculptor and grandson of an architect. As a boy, entered the workshop of a decorator and picture restorer, where he learned to draw by copying old paintings. Later studied at the Academy of Fine Arts in Rome under Aristide Sartorio. Since 1930 included in many of the principal Italian exhibitions. Associated with the *Novecento*, and during his middle career painted impressionistic landscapes and neo-classical figures. His most recent works are far more abstract than ever before. Has taught at the Academy of Fine Arts in Bologna; now lives in Venice.

* *Nude.* 1945. Oil on canvas. Lent by the artist. *Ill. pl. 75*

* *Figures in Space, III.* 1947. Oil on canvas. Lent by the artist. *Ill. pl. 76*

RENATO GUTTUSO

Born Palermo, Sicily, 1912. In 1931, determined to become a painter, moved to Rome where he has lived ever since, except for intervals in Milan and Sicily. Soon after arrival in Rome took part in a continuation of the "Roman School" of Scipione and Mafai, rebelling against *Novecento* classicism in collaboration with Cagli, Fazzini and others. Around 1939 active as painter and polemicist in the progressive *Corrente* movement of Milan. During the German occupation was active in the Resistance; in 1945 published book of bitterly anti-German drawings, *Gott Mit Uns.* In 1946 was member of the *Nuova secessione artistica italiana* which the following year became the *Fronte nuovo delle arti*—vanguard of mainly abstract painters and sculptors. Internationally the best known younger Italian painter and the dominant figure in his generation, Guttuso has been included in numerous major exhibitions at home and abroad.

* *Battle with Wounded Horses.* 1942. Oil on canvas, 18½ x 22⅞″. Lent by the Galleria Nazionale d'Arte Moderna, Rome. *Ill. pl. 106*

Beggars. c.1942. Oil on canvas, 20 x 16½″. The Museum of Modern Art, New York.

* *Artichoke and Apple.* 1946. Oil on canvas, 13¾ x 17¾″. Lent by the artist. *Ill. pl. 107*

* *Sleeping Carter.* 1946. Oil on canvas, 19¾ x 23⅝″. Lent by Dino Zanardo, Rome. *Ill. pl. 108*

Peppers. 1946. Watercolor, pen and ink, 19¾ x 26¾″. Lent by Mr. and Mrs. Laurance P. Roberts, Rome.

* *The Maffia.* 1948. Oil on canvas, 27⅝ x 35½″. The Museum of Modern Art, New York. *Color plate opp. p. 32*

Interior with Woman Sewing. 1949. Oil on canvas, 38¼ x 49¼″. Lent by the artist.

A group of recent drawings lent by the artist.

STANISLAO LEPRI

Born Rome, 1910, son of the Director of the Zoological Gardens in that city. Under family pressure, served in diplomatic service until dismissed by the Fascists during the recent war. With encouragement from Leonor Fini became a painter of fantastic subjects; designed sets and costumes for ballet, *Le Bal des blanchisseuses*, Paris, 1946. One-man shows: Rome (1945), Paris (1946), New York (1948).

* *Luncheon in the Tower.* 1945. Gouache on wood, 15¾ x 19¾″. Lent by The Hugo Gallery, New York. *Ill. pl. 104*

MARIO MAFAI

Born Rome, 1902. First exhibited in 1928 at *Club de Roma.* In 1930 showed with Scipione; this exhibition signalized the existence of the "Roman School" which reacted against *Novecento* formalism and proposed a neo-romanticism based on idiosyncratic and poetic conviction. Influential among younger artists throughout the 1930's. Has always worked in Rome. Noted for delicacy and sensitivity of his pictures of dried flowers and for his demolition scenes of Roman streets. Represented in many of the outstanding Italian exhibitions of the past fifteen years.

* *Landscape with Train.* 1928. Oil on wood, 11⅜ x 15⅜″. Lent by Ferrucio Asta, Milan. *Ill. pl. 92*

Still Life. c.1928. Oil on wood, 22½ x 15⅜″. Lent by Ferrucio Asta, Milan.

* *Dry Leaves and Carnations.* 1934. Oil on canvas, 27⅝ x 21¼″. Lent by Dr. Giulio Laudisa, Rome. *Ill. pl. 94*

Two Women Disrobing. 1935. Oil on canvas, 38⅝ x 31⅛″. Lent by the Galleria Nazionale d'Arte Moderna, Rome.

GIACOMO MANZÙ

Born Bergamo, 1908, of impoverished parents. Almost entirely self-taught as a sculptor, though studied informally at the Academy of Verona. In 1930 moved to Milan and attracted favorable notice in a group exhibition; still lives in that city. First representative one-man exhibition at Galleria della Cometa, Rome, 1938. During the war produced a series of courageous bas-reliefs of the Crucifixion, portraying one of the tormenting soldiers as a helmeted German. But his usual subjects are tender, romantic figures of women and adolescents. An intensely religious man, Manzù has also done a number of bronzes of Cardinals.

Awarded numerous prizes, culminating in the grand prize for Italian sculpture at the Venice Biennial Exposition of 1948.

* *Cardinal*. 1938. Bronze, 20½" high. Lent by the Galleria Nazionale d'Arte Moderna, Rome. *Ill. pl. 123*

Skeleton Hanging from the Cross. 1940. Bronze, 10⅝ x 15". Lent by Dr. Riccardo Gualino, Rome.

Cardinals and Deposition. 1941. Bronze, 15¾ x 21¼". Lent by Dr. Riccardo Gualino, Rome.

* *Christ and the German Soldier*. 1942. Bronze, 11¾ x 15¾". Lent by Dr. Riccardo Gualino, Rome. *Ill. pl. 124*

* *Portrait of a Lady*. 1946. Bronze, 68⅞" high. Lent by Mrs. Alice Lampugnani, Milan. *Ill. pl. 125*

Illustrations for *Le Georgiche di Virgilo*. Published 1948. Etchings. The Museum of Modern Art, New York.

A group of drawings lent by the artist.

MARINO MARINI

Born Pistoia, 1901. Lives in Milan. Studied painting and sculpture at the Academy of Fine Arts, Florence, under Domenico Trentacoste. Worked as painter and draftsman for a number of years. Often in Paris, 1928 to 1938; traveled widely in other European countries. Represented in numerous important exhibitions in Italy and abroad during the past twenty years. First prize for sculpture at the Roman Quadrennial Exposition of 1935 and again in a large exhibition in Paris in 1937. Considered by a majority of the leading Italian critics to be the outstanding sculptor of contemporary Italy. Now recognized abroad by a growing circle as one of the most vital sculptors of the younger European generation, both as portraitist and as the creator of large-scale figure pieces.

* *Prizefighter*. 1935. Bronze, 26½" high. Lent by Dr. W. R. Valentiner, Los Angeles. *Ill. pl. 117*

* *Nude*. 1943. Bronze, 52½" high. Lent by the Buchholz Gallery, New York. *Ill. pl. 118*

Portrait of Lamberto Vitali. 1945. Bronze, 8¹¹⁄₁₆" high. Private collection, Milan.

* *Horse and Rider*. 1947. Bronze, 64" high. Lent by Mrs. John D. Rockefeller III, New York. *Ill. pl. 119*

* *Portrait of Carlo Carrà*. 1947. Bronze, 9⅛" high. Lent by the artist. *Ill. pl. 121*

* *Horse and Rider*. 1948. Bronze, 38¼" high. The Museum of Modern Art, New York. *Ill. pl. 120*

A group of drawings lent by the artist.

ARTURO MARTINI

Born Treviso, 1889. Died 1947. As a youth was apprenticed to a ceramic workshop. Studied sculpture in Treviso and in Munich under Hildebrand. Visited Paris, 1911 and 1914. Mature career began around 1920. At this time his works

reproduced in the *scuola metafisica*'s magazine, *Valori Plastici*. During 1930's mainly at Milan; afterward taught sculpture at the Academy of Fine Arts, Venice. Violent and rather uncertain in temperament, he made expressive use of native sculptural styles, from the Etruscan to the Mannerist-Baroque. Given memorial recognition at the Venice Biennial Exposition of 1948.

* *Portrait of Chekhov*. 1919. Terra cotta, 17¾" high. Lent by Adriano Pallini, Milan. *Ill. pl. 115*

Women Chatting. Terra cotta. Lent by Count Contini Bonacossi, Florence.

* *Daedalus and Icarus*. 1934-35. Bronze, 24" high. Lent by Mrs. Brigida Martini, Rome. *Ill. pl. 116*

* *The Fisherman's Wife*. Terra cotta. Lent by Count Contini Bonacossi, Florence. *Ill. pl. 114*

MARCELLO MASCHERINI

Born Udine, 1906. Studied and lives in Trieste. Represented in numerous, important recent exhibitions in Italy, including the Quadrennial at Rome and the Biennial at Venice; awarded prizes in sculpture at Florence ("Donatello" competition, 1942) and Verona.

* *Cock*. 1948. Bronze, 19¾". Lent by the artist. *Ill. pl. 122*

AMEDEO MODIGLIANI

Born Livorno, 1884. Graduated from the local *lycée*, and decided to become an artist, at first more interested in sculpture than painting. Instructed in art by Micheli, a minor member of the *Macchiaioli*. Later also studied at the Academies of Florence and Venice. To Paris, 1906; first exhibited at *Salon des Indépendants* of 1908. Revisited Italy, 1909. Mature career in Paris began 1910, with climactic years 1915 to 1919. Influenced by Cézanne, Picasso and African sculpture. Aware of most advanced Parisian developments in art, but returned persistently to native sources—the Sienese primitives, Botticelli and the sixteenth-century Mannerists. Worked as sculptor as well as painter; superb draftsman. His early death in 1920 removed one of modern Italy's outstanding artists, one of the few whose international fame has grown more secure with the years.

* *Bride and Groom*. 1915-16. Oil on canvas, 21¾ x 18¼". The Museum of Modern Art, New York. Gift of Frederic Clay Bartlett. *Ill. pl. 53*

* *Head*. c.1915? Stone, 22¼" high. The Museum of Modern Art, New York. Gift of Mrs. John D. Rockefeller, Jr. in memory of Mrs. Cornelius J. Sullivan. *Ill. pl. 48*

Blaise Cendrars. 1916-17. Oil on composition board, 23¾ x 19⅝". Lent anonymously.

* *Jacques Lipchitz and His Wife*. 1916-17. Oil on canvas, 31½ x 21". Lent by The Art Institute of Chicago. Helen Birch Bartlett Memorial Collection. *Ill. pl. 52*

* *Reclining Nude.* 1918? Oil on canvas, 28¾ x 45¾″. Lent by Josef von Sternberg, Weehawken, N. J. *Ill. pl. 51*

* *Seated Nude.* 1918. Oil on canvas, 32½ x 26⅜″. Lent by Leigh B. Block, Chicago. *Ill. pl. 45*

* *The Servant.* 1919. Oil on canvas, 60 x 24″. Lent by the Albright Art Gallery, Buffalo, N. Y. Room of Contemporary Art. *Ill. pl. 46*

* *Caryatid.* c.1919. Stone, 36¼″ high. Lent by the Buchholz Gallery, New York. *Ill. pl. 47*

Beatrice Hastings. 1915. Pencil, 8½ x 5⅛″. Private collection, Milan.

Nude. 1915? Pencil, 21⅝ x 16¾″. Private collection, Milan.

Nude. 1915-16. Pencil, 21½ x 16 15/16″. Private collection, Milan.

Woman Sewing. 1916? Pencil, 16⅛ x 10¼″. Private collection, Milan.

Beata Matrex. 1916-17. Pencil, 21⅝ x 16 15/16″. Private collection, Milan.

Woman with a Hat. 1917. Pencil, 16⅝ x 9⅝″. Lent by Mr. and Mrs. Marcellin Castaing, Paris.

Head of a Woman. 1917. Pencil and watercolor, 15 x 9⅞″. Lent by Mr. and Mrs. Marcellin Castaing, Paris.

Lady with a Hat. 1918. Pencil, 21⅝ x 9⅞″. Private collection, Milan.

* *A Portrait of a Young Woman.* Pencil, 11⅛ x 7⅜″. Lent by the Fogg Museum of Art, Harvard University, Cambridge, Mass. Paul J. Sachs Collection. *Ill. pl. 49*

Man with a Beard. Pencil, 16⅜ x 9⅞. Lent by Sam A. Lewisohn, New York.

* *Man with a Hat.* 1920. Pencil, 19¼ x 12″. The Museum of Modern Art, New York. Given anonymously. *Ill. pl. 50*

GIORGIO MORANDI

Born Bologna, 1890. Today almost universally respected in Italy as that country's finest living painter. Studied at the Academy of Fine Arts in Bologna; has since lived there quietly, seldom leaving the city; has never been to Paris. In earliest professional years took Cézanne as his ideal, and determined upon exhaustive plastic research within a restricted iconographic range. Allied with the *scuola metafisica*, 1918-20, but worked independently. Later included in exhibitions of the *Novecento* group, and more recently represented in nearly all major Italian exhibitions; also shown abroad. Noted for his rare integrity and for the poetic as well as formal qualities of his art. Primarily a colorist, but also a fine print maker. Awarded first prize for Italian painting at the important Venice Biennial Exposition of 1948.

* *Still Life.* 1916. Oil on canvas, 32½ x 22⅝″. The Museum of Modern Art, New York. *Ill. pl. 57*

* *Still Life with Bottles and Fruit Dish.* 1916. Oil on canvas, 23⅝ x 21¼″. Lent by the Gianni Mattioli Foundation, Milan. Feroldi Collection. *Ill. pl. 58*

* *Flowers.* 1918. Oil on canvas, 32 5/16 x 26⅜″. Private collection, Milan. *Ill. pl. 59*

* *Still Life with Box and Ninepin.* 1918. Oil on canvas, 25⅝ x 21¼″. Lent by Riccardo Jucker, Milan. *Ill. pl. 42*

* *Mannequin on a Round Table.* 1918. Oil on canvas, 19¼ x 23¼″. Lent by Riccardo Jucker, Milan. *Ill. pl. 44*

* *Objects.* 1919. Oil on canvas, 20⅜ x 21¾″. Lent by Prof. Roberto Longhi, Florence. *Ill. pl. 43*

Still Life. 1920. Oil on canvas, 24 x 26⅜″. Private collection, Milan.

Still Life. 1920. Oil on canvas, 18⅛ x 15⅜″. Private collection, Milan.

Still Life. 1920. Oil on canvas, 11⅞ x 15¾″. Lent by the Galleria del Cavallino, Venice.

* *Still Life.* 1937. Oil on canvas, 17¾ x 23¼″. Lent by Viscount Dr. Franco Marmont, Milan. *Ill. pl. 62*

* *Landscape.* Oil on canvas. Lent by Dr. Pietro Rollino, Rome. *Ill. pl. 61*

* *Still Life.* 1939. Oil on canvas, 23½ x 31″. Lent by Dr. Pietro Rollino, Rome. *Color plate opp. p. 26*

Still Life. 1949. Oil on canvas, 13¾ x 10⅝″. Private collection, Milan.

Five etchings. The Museum of Modern Art, New York.

Landscape. 1913. 6⅜ x 9 3/16″.
Landscape. 1928. 9⅝ x 9¾″.
* *Landscape.* 1933. 8 1/16 x 11 13/16″. *Ill. pl. 60*
Still Life. 1933. 9 5/16 x 9 1/16″.
Still Life. 1934. 11⅝ x 15⅜″.

MARCELLO MUCCINI

Born, c. 1925. Allied with Vespignani and Graziella Urbinati in the very young Roman school which has returned to pre-twentieth-century sources and evolved a new romanticism, often marked by open pathos, but convincing in sincerity and talent. Muccini has outgrown his earlier dependence on Toulouse-Lautrec, and has progressed rapidly toward a personal style, both in his drawings and in his few completed paintings.

* *Bull.* 1948. Duco on plywood, 13 x 28¼″. The Museum of Modern Art, New York. *Ill. pl. 98*

* *Tragic Moment.* 1949. Charcoal, 17½ x 26″. Lent by Nelson A. Rockefeller, New York. *Ill. pl. 99*

FAUSTO PIRANDELLO

Born 1899, son of the playwright Luigi Pirandello. Self-taught as a painter. Spent two years in Paris and Berlin. One-man shows in Paris (1928) and Venice (1931); has also exhibited in Vienna and been included in several Quadrennial and Biennial Expositions at Rome and Venice respectively. Lives in Rome. His art is notable for its freshness of color and, despite its expressionist overtones, for a gracious relish of medium.

* *Bathers.* Oil on wood. Lent by Dr. Augusto Caraceni, Rome. *Ill. pl. 89*

Sunflowers. 1948. Oil on wood, 25¼ x 18½". Lent by the artist.

Goat's Head. 1948. Oil on wood, 18½ x 18½". Lent by the artist.

FILIPPO DE PISIS

Born Ferrara, 1896. Intensive literary studies in youth. Associated with de Chirico, Carrà and Savinio in the *scuola metafisica* at Ferrara, but primarily as a writer; published a book, *Pittura Moderna*, 1919, with material on the school. During 1920's decided on painting as career; since that time has spent many years in Paris, but has also worked at Venice. A prolific painter, he is related to French impressionism and post-impressionism, but also to the eighteenth-century Venetian tradition. Continues to write critical articles. Now lives in Venice.

Napoleon's Horse. 1924. Oil on canvas, 21⅝ x 18⅛". Lent by Cesare Tosi, Milan.

* *Still Life with Funnel and Shopping Bag.* 1925. Oil on cardboard, 20⅛ x 27³⁄₁₆". Lent by Viscount Dr. Franco Marmont, Milan. *Ill. pl. 77*

* *Poultry Yard.* 1928. Oil on wood, 16½ x 23". Lent by Dr. Giuseppe Vismara, Milan. *Ill. pl. 78*

* *The Door of My Studio.* 1935. Oil on canvas, 39¼ x 31½". Lent by Dr. Lionello Venturi, Rome. *Ill. pl. 79*

ARMANDO PIZZINATO

Born Maniago (Udine), 1910. Took courses in painting at the Academy in Venice. In 1932 began to exhibit; soon given one-man shows in Milan and Venice. Since 1940 has been awarded several important prizes in large Italian exhibitions. Fought in the Resistance and was arrested by the Fascists. Liberated in 1945, he resumed painting. Now a member of the *Fronte nuovo delle arti* with Guttuso, Santomaso and other younger Italian artists. Revives the Futurists' interest in kinetics. Lives in Venice.

* *Defenders of the Factory.* 1948. Oil on board, 26⅜ x 38⅝". Lent by the Galleria Internazionale d'Arte Moderna, Venice. *Ill. pl. 113*

Dockyards. 1948. Oil on canvas, 39¾ x 58¼". Lent by the artist.

OTTONE ROSAI

Born Florence, 1895. Studied briefly at the Institute of Decorative Art and at the Academy of Fine Arts in that city, but mainly self-taught. Joined the Futurist movement before the war; active as painter and ferocious polemicist. Fought in first World War. After the war had leading role in the magazine, *L'Universale.* Abandoned abstract painting for a realistic genre style, 1919-22, finding his subjects in the daily life of the poorer people of Florence; has continued to work in this manner, but in a more impressionistic spirit. Since 1920 has exhibited in all the principal cities of Italy and been included in numerous major exhibitions. Large one-man exhibition, Florence, 1945. Still lives in Florence, and teaches at its Academy of Fine Arts.

Still Life. 1919. Oil on canvas, 11⅞ x 15⁹⁄₁₆". Lent by A. Gonnelli, Florence.

* *Still Life with Powder Box.* 1919. Oil on canvas, 11⅞ x 15¾". Lent by Dr. Camillo Poli, Milan. *Ill. pl. 84*

The Card Players. 1920. Oil on canvas, 7½ x 9½". Lent by the Gianni Mattioli Foundation, Milan. Feroldi Collection.

* *My Father.* 1920. Oil on canvas, 12¼ x 10¼". Lent by the Gianni Mattioli Foundation, Milan. Feroldi Collection. *Ill. pl. 85*

* *Composition with a Priest.* 1920. Oil on canvas, 15¾ x 19¾". Lent by the Galleria del Cavallino, Venice. *Ill. pl. 86*

* *Billiard Players.* 1921. Oil on canvas, 10¼ x 11¼". Lent by A. Gonnelli, Florence. *Ill. pl. 83*

LUIGI RUSSOLO

Born near Venice, 1885. Original member of the Futurist group, and signed the artists' famous inaugural manifesto at Milan, 1910. Worked as painter and also interested in the musical side of Futurism; invented a "sound machine" on which the operator could produce those cacophonous

RUSSOLO: *The Revolt,* 1911. Not in the exhibition.

effects of scratching, thumping and clanking which the Futurists, with their emphasis on the esthetic validity of the machine, were anxious to incorporate in musical composition.

* *The Fog.* 1912. Oil on canvas. Lent by Donna Margherita Sarfatti, Rome. *Ill. pl. 17*

GIUSEPPE SANTOMASO

Born Venice, 1907. Traveled to Paris and northern Europe. First representative exhibition at Genoa, 1940. Admired Braque and Morandi, and is related in preoccupation with color to the Venetian tradition. Member of the *Fronte nuovo delle arti*. Lives in Venice.

* *Still Life with Chicken.* 1948. Oil on canvas, 23⅝ x 29½". Lent by the artist. *Ill. pl. 111*

* *Fisherman, No. 1.* 1948. Oil on canvas, 23⅝ x 35½". Lent by the artist. *Ill. pl. 112*

TOTI SCIALOJA

Born Rome 1914, and now lives there. Did not begin to paint seriously until around 1940, inspired by the expressionism of Soutine and, perhaps, of Scipione. An editor of the magazine, *L'Immagine*, with frequent articles on the newer tendencies in Italian art.

* *Factories on the Tiber.* 1946. Oil on canvas, 23⅝ x 27⅝". Lent by the artist. *Ill. pl. 96*

SCIPIONE (GINO BONICHI)

Born Macerata, 1904; died of tuberculosis, 1933. With Mario Mafai founded the "Roman School" which, beginning around 1928, achieved a vigorous revolt against the formalism of the *Novecento*, proposing a neo-romantic art based on direct experience and emotion in place of the older generation's neo-classicism and "primitivism." His sumptuous expressionist color and vivid sense of fantasy won him a leading place among younger Italian artists. His influence has increased rather than diminished since his early death, and he must be considered the outstanding single opponent of isolationist pomposity in the Italian art of his brief era. Given special memorial gallery at the Venice Biennial Exposition of 1948. Worked in Rome.

Study for *Portrait of the Senior Cardinal.* 1929. Oil on canvas, 19¾ x 17¾". Lent by the Gianni Mattioli Foundation, Milan. Feroldi Collection.

* *Still Life with Hat, Stick and Comb.* 1929. Oil on canvas, 23⅝ x 27⅝". Lent by the Galleria del Cavallino, Venice. *Ill. pl. 90*

* *Piazza Navona.* 1930. Oil on wood, 31⁵⁄₁₆ x 31¾". Lent by Princess Caetani di Bassiano, Rome. *Ill. pl. 91*

PIO SEMEGHINI

Born Quistello (Mantua), 1878. Lived much in Paris and Switzerland during earlier years. Represented in numerous public and private collections in Europe. Now lives in Verona.

Two oil paintings. Private collection, Milan.

GINO SEVERINI

Born Cortona, 1883. Moved to Rome, 1901. Met Boccioni and Balla around 1904. Worked in Paris. Signed the original *Manifesto of Futurist Painting* in 1910, but afterwards felt that the Futurist artists were too provincial and should see modern art, especially cubism, at its source in Paris. Showed with the Futurists for the first time in the Paris exhibition of February, 1912. Continuing to live in Paris, Severini was particularly interested in cabaret and nightclub subjects; was strongly influenced by Seurat's neo-impressionism, his color being consistently gayer than his colleagues'. Gradually abandoned Futurism during the war years, later adopted a neo-classic style. Active as a writer, his autobiography has recently appeared. Lives in Paris, with frequent trips to Italy.

* *Boulevard.* 1910-11. Oil on canvas, 25⅛ x 36⅛". Lent by Fred H. Mayor, London. *Ill. pl. 20*

Blue Dancer. 1912. Oil on canvas, 24⅜ x 18⅞". Lent by Romeo Toninelli, Milan.

* *Dynamic Hieroglyphic of The Bal Tabarin.* 1912. Oil on canvas with sequins, 63⅝ x 61½". The Museum of Modern Art, New York. *Ill. pl. 22*

* *Armored Train.* 1915. Oil on canvas, 46 x 34½". Lent by Mr. and Mrs. Charles J. Liebman, New York. *Ill. pl. 23*

* *Dancer—Helix—Sea.* 1915. Oil on canvas, 30½ x 29½".

SEVERINI: *Flying over Rheims* (see opposite page).

Lent by the Estate of Alfred Stieglitz, New York. *Ill. pl. 24*

* *The Train in the City.* 1913? Charcoal, 19⅝ x 25⅝". Lent by the Estate of Alfred Stieglitz, New York. *Ill. pl. 21*

* *Flying over Rheims.* 1915? Charcoal, 22⅜ x 18⅝". Lent by the Estate of Alfred Stieglitz, New York. *Ill. p. 134*

MARIO SIRONI

Born Sassari, 1885. Studied mathematics at the University of Rome, then decided to become a painter. Moved to Milan where he now lives. Took part in the Futurist movement, but soon reacted against "abstract" art. Painted several mannequin figures and very briefly was affected by the *scuola metafisica*, being sympathetic to the program of *Valori Plastici*. In 1926 was included in the exhibition of the *Novecento* at Milan. Developed a powerful romantic expressionism which seems highly personal. Executed commissions in fresco and mosaic during his middle career.

* *Urban Landscape.* 1929. Oil on canvas, 27⅝ x 31⅛". Lent by the Galleria del Cavallino, Venice. *Ill. pl. 68*

    Landscape. 1940. Oil on canvas, 19¾ x 23⅝". Lent by Cesare Tosi, Milan.

* *Light Spaces.* 1941. Tempera on canvas, 31⅞ x 24⅜". Lent by Carlo Frua de Angeli, Milan. *Ill. pl. 69*

* *The Flagellation.* 1948. Oil on canvas, 15¾ x 23⅝". Lent by Cesare Tosi, Milan. *Ill. pl. 70*

ARDENGO SOFFICI

Born Rignano sull'Arno, 1879. Began his studies in art at Florence, but moved to Paris at an early age; lived there seven years and was in contact with the most advanced artists of the *fauve* and cubist movements. In Italy aroused interest in the revolutionary developments of French painting. Associated with Futurism, 1913. Later became part of the *Novecento*'s reaction against "modern" art, but continued to interest his countrymen in the Parisian art scene. Active as a writer, and during the years immediately preceding the first World War was one of the most progressive critics in Europe. Now lives at Poggio a Cajano.

* *Still Life.* 1914. Oil and collage on canvas, 18⅛ x 15". Lent by Cesare Tosi, Milan. *Ill. pl. 30*

    Composition. 1915. Gouache, 17¾ x 14⅝". Lent by Riccardo Jucker, Milan.

GIOVANNI STRADONE

Born Nola, 1911. Lives in Rome, where he has been associated with Scialoja and others in the continuation of Scipione's expressionism, with particular, but well assimilated, reference to the art of Soutine.

* *The Colosseum.* 1945. Oil on canvas, 25⅝ x 19¾". Lent by Dr. Giulio Laudisa, Rome. *Ill. pl. 95*

ARTURO TOSI

Born Busto Arsizio, 1871. Lives in Milan, the dean of living Italian painters. Was associated with the *Novecento* from

its beginning, but to the neo-classicism of Funi and others opposed direct atmospheric naturalism with close affinities to both French and Lombard impressionism. Represented in many public and private collections in Italy. Awarded numerous prizes in major exhibitions.

* *San Giorgio Maggiore.* 1945. Oil on canvas, 19¾ x 23⅝". Lent by the artist. *Ill. pl. 64*

* *Still Life.* 1947. Oil on canvas, 19¾ x 15³⁄₁₆". Lent by the artist. *Ill. pl. 65*

    Autumn in Rovetta. 1948. Oil on canvas, 19¾ x 23⅝". Lent by Dr. Giuseppe Vismara, Milan.

RENZO VESPIGNANI

Born Rome, 1924. Now works in that city, and has become the best-known figure in the very young generation there, chiefly because of his remarkable drawings and prints. His melancholy, sensitive art is decidedly different from the aggressive painting of the *Fronte nuovo delle arti*, being closer in spirit to Toulouse-Lautrec's *fin de siècle* romanticism than to Picasso's brilliant dramaturgy. One-man shows in Rome, Milan, Stockholm and New York.

* *Ruined Building.* 1946. Pen and ink wash, 14¾ x 10¾". The Museum of Modern Art, New York. Purchase Fund. *Ill. pl. 100*

* *The Wall.* 1947. Pen and ink wash, 7½ x 18⅜". The Museum of Modern Art, New York. Purchase Fund. *Ill. pl. 101*

ALBERTO VIANI

Born Quistello, 1906. A sculptor-member of the *Fronte nuovo delle arti*, he now lives in Venice. Engrossed in subtle refinements of sculptural form, using a predominantly abstract and smoothly finished technique, Viani has taken part in the reappraisal of organic shapes begun in our century by Brancusi and others. Recently his sculpture has taken Jean Arp's biomorphic "concretions" as a point of departure.

* *Nude.* 1945. Marble, 39¾" high. Lent by Leone Traverso, Florence. *Ill. pl. 133*

GIUSEPPE VIVIANI

Born at Agnano di Pisa, 1898. Lives in Marina di Pisa. Especially notable as a graphic artist. Related in fantasy of imagination to the *scuola metafisica* and to surrealism. His mysteriously assorted objects are depicted in a prickly and exact technique which adds to their sense of shock and ambiguity.

* *The Leg.* 1939. Etching, 7¾ x 11⅞". The Museum of Modern Art, New York. *Ill. pl. 103*

    Bicycle by the Sea. 1941. Etching, 5½ x 8¾". The Museum of Modern Art, New York.

    Five miniature etchings. 1947. The Museum of Modern Art, New York.

Bibliography

All the following references are in the Museum Library (with a single and temporary exception) since it seemed apparent that the most functional bibliography should be based on material easily accessible and already here. The listing contains only a small portion of important periodicals like *Emporium*, which, however, are analyzed in detail in indexes such as the *Répertoire d'Art et d'Archéologie* and Wilson's *Art Index*.

Some effort has been made to locate material in various languages to suit the needs of different readers and to draw attention to books containing bibliographies. No effort has been made to document in full all the references on a single artist as this would exceed the requirements of this survey as established by the selection of artists and works in the exhibition itself. The entire literature on modern Italian art—recently acquired through the co-operation of Mr. Kenneth Donahue, formerly of the American Academy in Rome, and the friendly collaboration of the distinguished Italian critic, Mr. Lamberto Vitali—equals in extent the record below. For any serious research, the Library will make available an exhaustive bibliography of the known Italian literature, assembled by the art critic and master bibliographer Mr. Giovanni Scheiwiller.

In the compilation of this bibliography, special acknowledgment is made to Miss Mary Mitchell of the Library staff for her invaluable assistance.   BERNARD KARPEL

Abbreviations: [ ] bracketed information supplied by the compiler; Ap April; Ag August; bibl bibliographical reference so numbered; col colored; D December; ed editor, edition; F February; front frontispiece; il illustrated, illustrations; incl including; Ja January; Je June; Jy July; Mr March; My May; N November; n.d. not dated; n.p. not paged; no. nr. number; O October; p. page(s); pl plate(s); por portrait(s); S September; v volume(s).

Typical Entry: VITALI, LAMBERTO. Variaz oni metafisiche di Carrà. 4il Le Tre Arti 1no.3:3 D 1 1945, means that an article by Lamberto Vitali, titled Variazioni metafisiche di Carrà, containing 4 illustrations, will be found in Le Tre Arti, volume 1, number 3, page 3, issue dated December 1 1945.

General

1 LE ARTI BELLE (periodical). Numero speciale dedicato alla XXIV d'Venezia. 67p. il. Milano, 1948.
No. 14-15. Partial contents: Berto Lardera. L'arte astratta alla XXIV biennale.-Umbro Apollonio. La pittura metafisica alla XXIV biennale di Venezia.

2 BARBAROUX, VITTORIO E. & GIANI, GIAMPIERO. Arte italiana contemporanea. Prefazione di Massimo Bontempelli. [16]p. plus 150 pl. (some col.) Milano, Grafico S.A., 1940.

3 BERGAMO. INSTUTUTO ITALIANO D'ARTI GRAFICHE. La XXIV biennale di Venezia. 120p. il. Bergamo, 1948.
Brief bibliography. Includes articles from Emporium no. 613-14.

4 BODRERO, EMILIO. Dix années d'art en Italie, 1922-1932. il. Paris, Chroniques du Jour, n.d. (Collection Découverte du monde.2)
Useful only for a few plates on modern Italians.

5 BONFANTE, EGIDIO & RAVENNA, JUTI. Arte cubista. p.191-210 il. Venezia, Ateneo, 1945.
Partial contents: "Futuristi e indipendenti." "Scultori."

6 BRIZIO, ANNA MARIA. Ottocento, novecento. p.373-424 il. Torino, Editrice Torinese, 1939. (Storia universale dell'arte.6)
"La Scuola di Parigi: francesi, italiani stranieri," p.373-424. "La pittura in Italia," p.390-403. "Il futurismo—il novecento," p.404-24. "Scultori cubisti e futuristi," p.478-92. Bibliography.

7 CAIROLA, STEFANO, ed. Arte italiana del nostro tempo. 100 tavole a colori, 200 tavole in nero. Saggi critici . . . [130]p. plus 104 pl. (some col.) Bergamo, Instituto italiano d'arte grafiche, 1946.
Monumental anthology of painters and sculptors. Biographical sections include photograph of the artist, and text also accompanies each plate.

8 CARRÀ, CARLO. Il rinnovamento delle arti in Italia. 115p. plus 16 pl. Milano, Il Balcone, 1945. (Testi e documenti di arte moderna.)
Originally published in Valori Plastici, bibl. 23.

9 CARRIERI, RAFFAELE. Fantasia degli italiani. n.p. il. (some col.) Milano, Domus, 1939.
Special issue of "Domus." Includes excellent illustrations of some artists in this catalog. "Pittura metafisica (dinamismo plastico), plates 154-163 and elsewhere.

10 EICHMANN, INGEBORG. Letter from Italy: the Fronte nuove. il. Magazine of Art 42no2: 68-71 F 1949.
Cites manifesto, and refers in part to Guttuso, Santomaso, Viani and others.

11 FLORA, FRANCESCO. Dal romanticismo al futurismo. Nuova edizione con aggiunte. 415p. Milano, A. Mondadori, 1925.
"Il futurismo," p.67-102. "Ardengo Soffici," p. 261-66.

12 GERARD, HELEN. Italian notes. Magazine of Art 22no.5-23no.5: My 1931-My 1932.
News reports in the "Field notes" section.

13 IL MILIONE. Bollettino della galleria del Milione. no.1-73 (?) il. Milan, 1932-41.
Well-illustrated exhibition catalogs of the most progressive gallery in Italy during these years. Includes articles, biographies and bibliographies as well as current events.

14 LE NÉOCLASSICISME DANS L'ART CONTEMPORAIN. 96p. il. Rome, Valori plastici [1923]
Essays by Carlo Carrà and Ardengo Soffici. Includes reproductions of Carrà, de Chirico, Martini, Morandi, Soffici and others.

15 NEW YORK. MUSEUM OF MODERN ART. Cubism and abstract art. p.54-63, 205-7 et passim il. New York, 1936.
Text by Alfred H. Barr, Jr. Futurism, p.54-63; Boccioni, p.205; de Chirico, p.207,etc. Bibliography.

16 PAGANO, GIUSEPPE. Arte decorativa italiana. 142p. incl. il. Milano, Ulrico Hoepli, 1938. (Quaderni della Triennale.)
Includes paintings and sculpture by Cagli, Carrà, Campigli, Casorati, Fontana, Manzù, Martini, Sironi and others.

17 PAVOLINI, ALESSANDRO & PONTI, GIOVANNI. Le arte in Italia, volume primo. n.p. il. Milano, Domus, 1938.
Special issue of "Domus." Includes some artists represented in this catalog.

18 PODESTÀ, ATTILIO. Bilancio della rassegna nazionale di arti figurative. il. Emporium 107no.641:195-210 My 1948.

19 ——— Il padiglione italiano e la partecipazione straniera. il. Emporium 108no.613-14:79-104 Jy-Ag 1948.
Partial contents: La mostra della metafisica e la retrospettive italiane. La pittura contemporanea italiana. La scultura contemporanea italiana. Also published in bibl. 3.

20 Portfolio IV. n.p. il. Rome, Black Sun press, 1945?
Italian number of "Portfolio" (U.S.), edited by Caresse Crosby. Issued in numbered leaflets, loose in folio. Contains illustrations of work by Morandi, Carrà, de Chirico, Guttuso, Manzù, Fazzini, Scipione, Afro, Cagli, Campigli and others. Foreword by the editor, article on painting by Ragghiante, and extract from de Chirico's memoirs.

21 ROMERO BREST, JORGE. Artistas italianos de hoy. il. Saber Vivir (Buenos Aires) 7no.73:34-7 1947.
The author has also written "La pintura italiana" (6 no63:44-5 1946) and "El arte italiano contemporaneo" (6no64:24-9 1946).

22 SCHEIWILLER, GIOVANNI. Art italien moderne. 93p. incl. 92il. Paris, Bonaparte, 1930.
Preface, p.7-19. Bibliography, p.20-22. Reproductions, p.24-87.

23 VALORI PLASTICI. Direttore: Mario Broglio. il. 1no.1-3 no.5 N15 1918-O 1921.
Invaluable record of the metaphysical group, with articles by and on de Chirico, Carrà, Soffici and others. Good plates.

24 VISENTINI, GINO. Gusti esagerati. 170p. plus 32 pl. Firenze, Vallecchi, 1942.
Essays on Scipione, Morandi, Manzù, as well as others.

25 ZUFFI, PIETRO, ed. Arte contemporaneo italiano. Textos de Raffaele Carrieri, Libero de Libero, G. di San Lazzaro, Nicola Ciarletta. [20]p. plus pl. (some col.) Santiago de Chile, Los Talleres Zig-zag, 1946.
Essays in Spanish and Italian on painting, sculpture, drawing. Bibliography.

Exhibitions

26 BERNE, KUNSTHALLE. Moderne italienische Kunst. 42p. 1947.
Exhibition of 370 works held Mr 22-Ap 13. Preface by Michele Biancale. Brief biographical notes.

27 CAIRO. PALAIS ISMAIL PACHA, KISR EL NIL. Exposition de peinture moderne italienne depuis 1850 jusqu'à nos jours. Organisée par la Société des amis de l'art du Caire et par la Biennale de Venise. 52p. plus 18 il. Venise, Editions Serenissima, 1949.
Exhibition held February-March. Introductions by N. Barbantini and U. Apollonio. Includes decorative arts as well as painting and sculpture.

28 CATANIA. MOSTRA D'ARTE CONTEMPORANEA. 40 anni d'arte italiana. Mostra degli artisti siciliani. Catalogo. 73p. plus 32 il. Catania, Palermo, 1949.
Exhibition held February-April. Includes biographical notes.

29 LUCERNE. KUNSTMUSEUM. 40 Jahre italienischer Kunst. 40p. il. 1947.
Exhibit organized by the Biennale di Venezia, held March 29-June 1. Contents: Carlo Carrà, "Futurisme."—Sergio Solmi, "La peinture metaphysique."—Giuseppe Marchiori, "Le novecento," and "Les

tendances actuelles."—Domenico Cantatore, "Gravures, lithographies et dessins."

30 MADRID. MUSEO NACIONAL DE ARTE MODERNO. Exposición de arte italiano contemporáneo. 44p. il. [Milan, Galleria del Cavallino de Venezia, 1948]
Exhibit held May, under the auspices of the Galleria del Cavallino. Preface by M. Bonini. Includes brief biographical sections on Scipione, Campigli, Carrà, Casorati, de Chirico, de Pisis, Guidi, Guttuso, Mafai, Manzù, Marini, Martini, Modigliani, Morandi, Rosai, Sironi, Tosi and others.

31 NEW YORK. COMETA ART GALLERY. Anthology of contemporary Italian painting. 39p. incl. il. New York, 1937.
Introduction, p.7. Plates, p.11-37, including one each of Afro, Cagli, Guttuso, Mafai, Pirandello and others.

32 ROME. PRIMA QUADRIENNALE D'ARTE NAZIONALE. Catalogo. il. Romà, 1931.
Includes sections on each of the following, with statement by the artist: Tosi, p.29-31; Soffici, p.46-50; Carrà, p.51-3; Casorati, p.74-8, Sironi, p.113-15.

33 ROME. GALLERIA DEL SECOLO. 25 artisti del secolo alla galleria del Secolo. [69]p. incl. 12 il. Rome, 1944.
Exhibit held Nov. 9-Dec. 15. Preface by Carlo Belli, p.7-28. English insert [5p.] "Modern Italian art." One of a series of excellent catalogs and bulletins issued by the gallery.

34 ZURICH. KUNSTHAUS. Italienische Maler. Katalog mit Bibliographie und Abbildungen. 32p. plus 16pl. 1927.
Exhibit held March 18-May 1. Preface by W. Wartmann. Bibliography, p.14-32, including Borra, Campigli, Carrà, Casorati, de Chirico, Donghi, Modigliani, de Pisis, Sironi, Tosi and the "Novecento italiano." Reviewed by Giedion in Der Cicerone 19nr.13:418-20 Jy 1927.

35 VENICE. BIENNALE. Catalogo. il. 24v. Venice, 1897-1948.
A record of the international exhibitions with sections on Italian art. Only the more recent annuals deal with artists of interest in this catalog.

Painting

36 ALBINI, MARIA-BRANDON. Nouvelles orientations de la peinture italienne. il. Arts de France no.11-12:57-65 1947.

37 ARCANGELI, FRANCESCO. Sulla pittura metafisica: Carrà, de Chirico, Morandi. 2il. Vernice (Trieste) 32p. 22-23: 24 Ap-My 1948.

38 ARGAN, CARLO GIULIO. Peinture italienne et peinture européenne. il. Les Arts Plastiques. no.5-6:204-13 1948.

39 BONFANTE, EGIDIO. Considerazione sulla pittura italiana dei giovani. 100p. il. Milano, G.G. Görlich, 1945.

40 BRANDI, CESARE. Su alcuni giovani: Afro, Mafai, Manzù, Mirco. p.[287-93] il. Firenze, Felice Le Monnier, 1939.
Extract from "Le Arti," 1no.3 F-Mr 1939.

41 BULLIET, C. J. The significant moderns. p.73-77, 127-29, 188-94 il. New York, Covici-Friede, 1936.
Sections on Modigliani, de Chirico, and the Italians (Balla, Severini, Carrà).

42 CARRÀ, CARLO. De l'état de la peinture italienne. In Le Néoclassicisme dans l'art contemporain. p.38-43 Rome, Valori plastici [1923]

43 ——— Pittura metafisica. 2a. ed. riv. 264p. Milano, Il Balcone, 1945.(Testi e documenti di arte moderna. 1)

44 CARRIERI, RAFFAELE. Otto pittori italiani contemporanei: Campigli, Carrà, Cesetti, de Chirico, Morandi, Soffici, Tomea, Tosi. [6]p. plus 11 col. pl. Milano, Stabilimento Grafico, 1940.
Paintings from the Marmont collection.

45 COSSIO DEL POMAR, FELIPE. Nuevo arte. p.132-4, 173-5 il. Buenos Aires, La Facultad, 1934.
On "futurismo," "valori plastici" and "Chirico."

46 COSTANTINI, VINCENZO. Pittura italiana contemporanea, dalla fine dell' 800 ad oggi. 435p. il. Milano, Ulrico Hoepli, 1934.
"Dizionarietto degli artisti contemporanei," p.387-423.

47 DAÜBLER, THEODOR. Moderne Italiener. il. Das Kunstblatt 5nr.2:49-53 1921.

48 ―――― Neueste Kunst in Italien. il. Der Cicerone 12nr. 9:349-54 My 1920.
Refers to Soffici, de Chirico, Carrà and others.

49 DORFLES, GILLO. Italian artists at the XXIV Venice biennale. il. Studio 137no.672:84-85 Mr 1949.

50 EINSTEIN, CARL. Die Kunst des 20. Jahrhunderts. 2. Aufl. p.46-7, 101-13, 231-5, 342-52, 558, 562. Berlin, Propyläen Verlag, 1928.
"Amedeo Modigliani," "Der Futurismus" (Boccioni, Severini, Carrà, de Chirico). Biographical notes and illustrations.

51 GRADA, RAFFAELE DE. Figurative art in Italy. Il'45 (Milan) 1no.1:7-14 F 1946, 1no.3:3-6 My 1946.
Part 1: At the origins of fascism. 2: "Novecento," the century's rest. Also "Fascism and art," 1no.1:5-6 F 1946.

52 HUYGHE, RENÉ, ed. Histoire de l'art contemporain: la peinture. Publiée sous la direction de René Huyghe. . . avec le concours de Germain Bazin. p.469-91 il. Paris, Félix Alcan, 1935.
Chapitre XVIII: Les Pays Latins: "Introduction" par René Huyghe, p.469-74. "L'Italie et le futurisme" par Gino Severini, p.475-78. "Notice historique sur le futurisme," par Vergnet-Ruiz, p.478-80. "Bibliographie générale de la peinture italienne," [bibliographie futuriste] [notices sur Balla, Boccioni, Severini], p.480-82. "La peinture italienne après le futurisme" par Vincenzo Costantini, p.483-88. "Notices" [Campigli, Carrà, Casorati, de Chirico, de Pisis, Rosai, Sironi, Soffici, Tosi, and others] p.488-91. Previously published in L'Amour de l'Art 15:469ff N 1934. See also bibl. 196.

53 KAINES-SMITH, J. C. The Italian school. In his An outline of modern painting in Europe and America. p.162-72 New York, William Morrow [1931?]

54 LISSITSKY, EL & ARP, HANS. Die Kunstismen. 11p. plus 48 pl. Erlenbach-Zürich, München und Leipzig, Eugen Rentsch, 1925.
Cover-title: Kunstism, 1914-1924. Text in German, French, English, including statement on the metaphysicians, and on futurism (Boccioni). Illustrations of de Chirico, Carrà, Boccioni, Severini, Balla.

55 MELTZOFF, STANLEY. Italy: report on recent painting. il. Magazine of Art 39no.2:52-57 F 1946.
An evaluation, with specific commentary on de Chirico, Severini, de Pisis, Morandi, Guttuso and others.

56 Modern Italian painters. [4]p. plus 15 col. pl. Englewood, H. Felix Kraus, 1947.

57 NEBBIA, UGO. La pittura del novecento. 2a. ed. p.97-310 il. Milano, Societa editrice libraria, 1946.
"Parte seconda: Il novecento italiano."

57aPISIS, FILIPPO DE. La cosidetta "arte metafisica." 9 il. Emporium 88no.527:257-65 N 1938.

58 Pittori italiani contemporanei. 50 pl. n.d. [1948?]
A scrapbook of mounted photographs.

59 RAGGHIANTI, CARLO L. Contemporary Italian painting. il. (1 col.) In Portfolio IV: folded leaf 1945?
Includes Morandi, de Pisis, Carrà, de Chirico, etc. See bibl. 19.

60 SARTORIS, ALBERTO. La pintura en Italia. 9 Artes (Buenos Aires) no.3:29, 31-2 Je 1948.

61 ―――― La pittura nella scuola moderna di Milano. 89p. incl. il. Como, Azienda autonoma di soggiorno e turismo, 1937.
Plates, p.13-80.

62 VENTURI, LIONELLO. Pittura contemporanea. p.34-35, 47-50 il.(some col.) Milano, Ulrico Hoepli [1947]
"Futuristi." "Morandi e altri italiani."

63 ―――― Pittura italiana contemporanea in una mostra a Londra. il. Emporium 104no.620:51-7 Ag 1946.

Sculpture

64 BARGELLINI, PIERO. Scultura italiana contemporanea. Sessanta tavole—con una ragione critica e un' antologia di guidizi a cura dell' editore. xix, 94p. incl. il. Firenze, Arnaud, 1945.
Sections on Fazzini, Manzù, Marini, Martini, Mascherini and others.

65 CAIROLA, STEFANO, ed. Arte italiana del nostro tempo. Bergamo, 1946.
See bibl. 7. Sections on Fazzini, Fontana, Marini, Martini, Manzù, Viani and others.

66 CAROSSO, F. Italiaanse plastieke. il. Kroniek van Kunst en Kultuur 9no.2:33-40 F 1948.
Includes Fazzini, Fontana, Marini, Martini, Manzù, Mascherini and others.

67 PODESTÀ, ATTILIO. La scultura contemporanea italiana. In Bergamo. Instituto italiano d'arti grafiche. La XXIV biennale di Venezia. p.96-104 il. Bergamo, 1948.

68 SARTORIS, ALBERTO. La escultura en Italia. 9 Artes (Buenos Aires) no.2:11,18 D 1947.

See also MONOGRAPHS section on Boccioni, Fazzini, Fontana, Manzù, Marini, Martini, Viani.

Graphic Art

69 CARRIERI, RAFFAELE. Il disegno italiano contemporaneo. 39p. plus 70 pl. (some col.) Milano, Enrico Domiani, 1945 (I disegnatori italiani. 2)
Includes Modigliani, Boccioni, Carrà, de Chirico, Sironi, Casorati, Campigli, Marini, de Pisis, Scipione, Morandi, Manzù and others.

70 RUOTA, ATTILIO. Contemporary Italian engravers. il. Graphis 3no.19:176-83, 248 1947.
Text also in French and German.

70aVENTUROLI, MARCELLO. Queste acqueforti. [Roma, C.I.R., 1947]
Signed prints, loose in folio. On cover: 6 acqueforti di Muccini, Urbinato, Vespignani. Museum copy has original drawing on inside cover by Vespignani.

71 VITALI, LAMBERTO. L'incisione italiana moderna. 146p. plus 52 il. Milano, Ulrico Hoepli, 1934.
Extensive bibliography, p.123-34. Essays on "L'incisione italiana" appeared as a series in "Domus" (Milan) from 1930-1932.

See also bibl. 104, 111, 121, 154, 169, 174, 183, 211, 222, 237, 239.

Futurism

72 BERNHEIM-JEUNE, GALERIE, PARIS. Les futuristes italiens. [8]p. incl. il. Paris, 1935.
Exhibition held April 3-27. Texts by Prampolini, Marinetti, etc.

73 BOCCIONI, UMBERTO. Pittura, scultura futuriste (dinamismo plastico). il. [472]p., front.(por.), plus 51 pl. Milano, Edizioni futuriste di "Poesia," 1914.

74 CARRÀ, CARLO. Guerra pittura, futurismo politico, dinamismo plastico. il. 104p. Milano, Edizioni futuriste di "Poesia," 1915.

75 CHENEY, SHELDON. The story of modern art. p.466-73 il. New York, Viking press, 1940.

76 CLOUGH, ROSA TRILLO. Looking back at futurism. 207p. New York, Cocce press, 1942.
Thesis on the writings of the futurists. Bibliography, p.205-7.

77 COQUIOT, GUSTAVE. Cubistes, futuristes, passéistes. 3.ed. p.63-94, 205-37 il. Paris, Ollendorf, 1914.
On the futurist painters and Boccioni.

78 EDDY, ARTHUR JEROME. Futurism. *In his* Cubists and post-impressionism. Rev. ed. p.164-90 il. Chicago, A.C. McClurg, 1919.
Bibliography.

79 FILLIA. Il futurismo: ideologie, realizzazione & polemiche del movimento futurista italiano. 125p. Milano, Sonzogno, 1932 (Biblioteca del popolo).
Bibliography.

80 HUYGHE, RENÉ, ed. Histoire de l'art contemporaine: la peinture. p.469-91 il. Paris, Félix Alcan, 1935.
See bibl. 52. Originally published in L'Amour de l'Art 15: 469 N 1934. Especially articles by Gino Severini, historical summary by Vergnet-Ruiz and extensive bibliographies on the movement and its artists, p.480-82, 488-91.

81 LACERBA. Direttore: Giovanni Papini. 1no.1-3 no.22 Firenze, Ja 1 1913-My 22 1915.
A futurist journal. Manifestes by Papini, Marinetti, etc. Writings and reproductions of Boccioni, Carrà, Soffici, Rosai, Russolo, etc., including prints, drawings.

82 MARINETTI, FILIPPO TOMMASO. Le futurisme. 238p. Paris, E. Sansot, n.d.
"Manifestes et proclamations futuristes," p.137-238.

83 DER STURM. Edited by H. Walden. Berlin, 1912-13.
Manifestoes, illustrations and other items by and on the futurists appeared in these numbers: 101,104 *Mr 1912*; 105, 107 *Ap 1912*; 110, 111 *My 1912*; 112 *Je 1912*; 132, 133 *O 1912*; 136, 137 *N 1912*; 150,151 *Mr 1913*; 172, 173 *Ag 1913*; 190, 191 *D 1913*. The second exhibition of Der Sturm was futurist, and a "Manifest der Futuristen" appeared in no. 101: 822-24 Mr 1912.

84 ZERVOS, CHRISTIAN. Le futurisme. *In his* Histoire de l'art contemporaine. p. 355-62 incl il. Paris, Cahiers d'Art, 1938.
Plates, p.356-62.

Monographs and Critiques

AFRO

85 PITTINI, FRED. Afro, Taiuti, Pittino. 1il Il Milione (Milan) no.7: [1] Ja 24—F 5 1933.
"Bollettino della galleria del Milione."

86 [Afro] *In* Brandi, Cesare. Su alcuni giovani. See bibl. 40.

BALLA

87 [Balla: Notice biographique et bibliographique] *In*

Huyghe, René. Histoire de l'art contemporaine: la peinture. p.481 il Paris, Félix Alcan, 1935.
Originally published in L'Amour de l'Art 15:481 N 1934.

88 BOCCIONI, UMBERTO. Pittura, scultura futuriste . . . con 51 reproduzioni . . . di Boccioni, Carrà, Russolo, Balla, Severini, Soffici. 5 il. Milano, Edizioni futuriste di "Poesia," 1914.

89 BULLIET, C. J. Giacomo Balla. *In his* The significant moderns. p.188-91 2il New York, Covici-Friede, 1936.

BARTOLINI

89aBERTOCCHI, NINO. Luigi Bartolini. Testo per la pittura: Nino Bertocchi, per l'acquaforte: C.A. Petrucci. [24]p. plus 22 pl.(some col.) Torino, Chiantore [1945?] (Artisti italiani contemporanei.)
Bibliography included in Gino Visentini *Bartolini* p.35-7, Rovereto, Delfino, 1943.

BOCCIONI

90 BOCCIONI, UMBERTO. Manifeste technique de la sculpture futuriste. Bulletin de L'Effort Moderne no. 15: 11-13 My 1925.
Signed "Milan, 11 avril 1912."

91 ——— Pittura, scultura futuriste (dinamismo plastico). il [472]p front.(por.), plus 51 pl. Milano, Edizioni futuriste di "Poesia," 1914.

92 ——— Simultanéité futuriste. Der Sturm (Berlin) 4nr.190-1:151 D 1913.
Boccioni quotes from the first manifesto on futurist painting (April 11, 1910), the catalog of the first exhibition in Paris (Galerie Bernheim, Feb. 5, 1912), the manifesto of futurist sculpture (Apr. 11, 1912), the catalog of the first exhibition of futurist sculpture (Galerie La Boëtie, June 1913).

93 COQUIOT, GUSTAVE. Boccioni. *In his* Cubistes, futuristes, passéistes. 3.ed. p.205-37 il. Paris, Ollendorf, 1914.

94 SOBY, JAMES THRALL. Italy: Two movements and two paintings. il. Magazine of Art 39:49-51,76-9 F 1946.

95 WALDEN, HERWARTH. Umberto Boccioni. *In his* Einblick in Kunst. p.142 2il. Berlin, Verlag Der Sturm, 1924.

See also bibl. 72-84.

BORRA

96 BORRA, POMPEO. Pittura astratta. [16]p. incl. 6 il. Milano, Edizioni Bergamini, n.d.

97 BERGAMINI GALLERIA, MILAN. Bollettino, arte e lettere. no. 1-8 Milano, 1946-48.
The bulletins contain contributions by Borra in almost every issue. Library has no. 1-7/8 1946-Ja-F/1948.

98 IL MILIONE, GALLERIA, MILAN. Il Milione, no. 51 [Borra issue] [12]p. incl. il. Milan, 1937.
Catalog for exhibition held F 18-Mr 5. Includes reviews and bibliography.

99 JOPPOLO, BENIAMINO. Pompeo Borra. *In* Cairola, Stefano, ed. Arte italiana del nostro tempo. p.9-10 il (por.) Bergamo, Instituto italiano d'arte, 1946.

100 SCHEIWILLER, GIOVANNI. Pompeo Borra. [94]p. incl. 58 pl. (some col) Milano, Conchiglia [1941]
Text in Italian and German. Biographical and bibliographical notes in pictorial section.

CAGLI

101 CAGLI, CORRADO. Muri ai pittori. 2il. Quadrante no.1: 19 My 1933.
Commentary by A. Spaini, p.19-20. Additional drawing, p.22; brief note, p.23. Later, the artist wrote "Lettere a Quadrante" on the murals of the Triennale in no. 3: 46-7 Jy 1933.

102 BARDI, P. M. 3 giovani pittori romani: Cagli, Capogrossi, Cavalli, 3il. Il Milione (Milan) no.9:2-4 F 21-Mr 5 1933.
"Bollettino della galleria del Milione." Biographical note.

103 BONTEMPELLI, MASSIMO. Corrado Cagli. 22p. plus 16 pl. Roma, Studio d'arte Palmà, 1947.

104 OLSON, CHARLES. Y & X. Drawings by Corrado Cagli, poems by Charles Olson. 12 folding leaves 5 il. Black Sun press, 1948.
Issued loose in box.

105 [LOUCHHEIM, ALINE B.] Spotlight on Cagli. il (por.) Art News 46no.2:26,58, Ap 1947.

106 WINDHAM, DONALD. A dark riddle illustrated for View by Corrado Cagli. View (New York) 6no.3:6 My 1946.

CAMPIGLI

107 CARRIERI, RAFFAELE. Campigli. 128p. incl. il. (some col.) Venezia, Cavallino, 1945.
Biographical and bibliographical note, p.19-28, includes reviews as well as commentary by the artist.

108 COURTHION, PIERRE. Massimo Campigli. 9p. plus 36 pl. Paris, Chroniques du Jour, 1938. (Art italien moderne. 6)

109 FRANCHI, RAFFAELO. Massimo Campigli. 27p. plus 35 il. (col. front.) Milan, Ulrico Hoepli, 1944. (Arte moderna italiana, 20)
Extensive bibliography, p.18-27.

110 RAYNAL, MAURICE. Campigli. 30p., 13 il., plus 24 col. pl. Paris, Jeanne Bucher, 1949.
Cover-title: Peintures 1928-1948. Biographical and bibliographical note, p.29-30. Printed in Milan. Raynal also issued "12 opere di Massimo Campigli" [6]p., frontis., plus 12 col.pl. Milano Il Milione, 1948.

111 SOLMI, SERGIO. Campigli litografo. 3il. Le Tre Arti 2no.2:5 F 1946.

CARRÀ

112 CARRÀ, CARLO. La mia vita. 2.ed. 372p. Milano, Rizzoli, 1943 (Il Cammeo.II)
Partial contents: Alle soglie del futurismo. La mia esperienza futurista. Pittura metafisica.

113 BARDI, P.M. Carrà e Soffici, 102 tavole e referenze. 46p. plus 102 il. Milano, Belvedere, 1930.

114 CATALANO, SILVIO. 12 opere di Carlo Carrà. [14]p. plus 12 col. pl. Milano, Il Milione, 1945. (Pittori italiani contemporanea.)
"Con una dichiarazione dell'artista."

115 GEORGE, WALDEMAR. From "pittura metafisica" to classic realism: Carlo Carrà. 4il Formes no.30:330 plus pl. 1932.

116 LONGHI, ROBERTO. Carlo Carrà. 2.ed. 43p., col. front., plus 37 pl. Milano, Ulrico Hoepli, 1945. (Arte moderna italiana. 11)
Extensive bibliography, p.21-43.

117 PACCHIONI, GUGLIELMO. Carlo Carrà. 75p. plus 75 pl. (some col.) Milano, Il Milione, 1945.
Extensive bibliography, p.58-71.

118 SOFFICI, ARDENGO. Carlo Carrà. 14p., col. front., plus 29 il. Milano, Ulrico Hoepli, 1928.
Bibliography, p.13-14.

119 TORRIANO, PIERO. Carlo Carrà. [18]p., front. (por.), plus 50 pl. (some col.) Milano, Garzanti, 1942. (Monografie d'arte di "Stile.")
Extensive bibliography, [8]p.

120 VITALI, LAMBERTO. Variazioni metafisiche di Carrà. 4il Le Tre Arti 1no.3:3 D 1 1945.

CASORATI

121 CASORATI, FELICE. Dieci litografie. 10 pl. Torino, Stabilimento grafica impronta, 1946. (Collezione del bibliofilo.)
Ten signed lithographs in folio. Edition of 100 copies, also five containing an original drawing.

122 CREMONA, ITALO. Felice Casorati. [10]p. plus 19 pl. (some col.) Torino, Accame,n.d. (Artisti italiani contemporanei.)

123 GALVANO, ALBINO. Felice Casorati. 2.ed. 55p., col. front., plus 34 pl. Milano, Ulrico Hoepli, 1947. (Arte moderna italiana. 5)
Extensive bibliography, p.41-54.

124 SALINGER, MARGARETTA M. The classic Casorati. 1il Parnassus 5no.1:20-2 Ja 1933.

125 SOLMI, SERGIO. Visita allo studio di Casorati 2il. (col.) Lettere ed Arti 2no.3:16-21 Mr. 1946.

CASSINARI

125aGRADA, RAFFAELE DE. A "new" painter: Bruno Cassinari. 4il.(2 col.) Il'45(Milan) 1no.2:3-8 Ap 1946.

DE CHIRICO

126 DE CHIRICO, GIORGIO. Sull'arte metafisica. Valori Plastici 1no.4-5:15-18 Ap-My 1919.
Typical of the many articles by de Chirico in bibl. 23. Reprinted in bibl. 130.

127 —— Statues, meubles et généraux. Bulletin de L'Effort Moderne. no.38:3-6 O 1927.

128 —— Sur le silence. Minotaure no.5:31-2 My 1934.

129 —— Sensitiveness. Horizon 10 no.55:65-68 Jy 1944.

130 —— Commedia dell' arte moderna, di Giorgio de Chirico e di Isabella Far. Roma, Nuove edizione italiane, 1945.
"Scritti di Giorgio de Chirico" (1918-1943), p.7-127. Essays include "Noi metafisica," "Il ritorno al mestiere," "Estetica metafisica" and others.

131 —— Memorie della mia vita. 257p. Roma, Astrolabio, 1945.

132 FALDI, ITALO. Il primo de Chirico. 26p., front.(por.) plus 32 pl. Venezia, Alfieri, 1949. (Arte d'oggi).
Bibliography, p.24-6.

133 GAFFÉ, RENÉ. Giorgio de Chirico, le voyant. 42p., front. (por.), plus 23 pl. Bruxelles, La Boétie, 1946.

134 GEORGE, WALDEMAR. Chirico, avec des fragments littéraires de l'artiste. 20p. plus 30 pl. Paris, Chroniques du Jour, 1928. (Les maîtres nouveaux.)

135 GOODRICH, LLOYD. Giorgio de Chirico. il. The Arts 15no.1:5-10 Ja 1929, 17no.11:110-13 N 1930.

136 LO DUCA, GIUSEPPE. Dipinti di Giorgio de Chirico (1912-1932). 2.ed. 41p., col. front., plus 37 pl. Milano, Ulrico Hoepli, 1945.
Extensive bibliography, p.17-41. First edition, 1936.

137 PICA, AGNOLDOMENICO. 12 opere di Giorgio de Chirico. [18]p., 5il. (2 col.) plus 14 col. pl. Milano, Il Milione, 1944. (Pittori italiani contemporanei.)
"Terza edizione" contains minor variations.

138 SOBY, JAMES THRALL. The early Chirico. 120p., col. front., plus 69 pl. New York, Dodd, Mead, 1941.
Extensive bibliography, p.113-16, supplements Lo Duca (1936 edition).

CLERICI

138a[PONTI, LISA?] Orpheus di Igor Strawinsky . . . Fabrizio Clerici, costumi e scene. 14 il. Domus 6no.231:27-9 1948.

DONGHI

139 SINISGALLI, LEONARDO. Antonio Donghi. 16p., col. front., plus 36 pl. Milano, Ulrico Hoepli, 1942. (Arte moderna italiana. 42)
Extensive bibliography, p.11-16.

140 CAIROLA, STEFANO. Antonio Donghi. *In his* Arte italiana del nostro tempo. p.32-33 il (por.) Bergamo, Instituto italiano d'arte grafiche, 1946.
See bibl. 7.

FAZZINI

141 BARGELLINI, PIERO. Pericle Fazzini. *In his* Scultura italiana contemporanea. p.15-19 3il. Firenze, Arnaud, 1945.
Biographical and autobiographical statement.

142 GUZZI, VIRGILIO. Pericle Fazzini. *In* Cairola, Stefano, ed. Arte italiana del nostro tempo. p. 34-35 il.(por.) Bergamo, Instituto italiano d'arte grafiche. 1946.
Also published, in part, in Arte Contemporanea 2no.9-10:3 N-D 1947.

143 RICAS, RICCARDO. Fazzini: due sculture e la posizione del pubblico. il. Domus no.226:39 1948.

144 ROSENDORFSKY, JAROSLAV. Pericle Fazzini. 1il. Blok (Brno) 2no.2:64 1947.
Brief note.

145 RUDOFSKY, BERNARD. Pericle Fazzini, sculptor. 12 il (por.) Interiors 108:106-11 D 1948.

FIUME

145aBORROMINI, GALLERIA, ROME. Salvatore Fiume. [12]p. incl. il.(por.) 1949.

FONTANA

146 MOROSINI, DUILIO. Lucio Fontana: 20 disegni con una prefazione. 21p. plus 20 pl. Milano, Corrente, 1940.
Bibliography, p.20-21.

147 PODESTÀ, ATTILIO. Genova: le ceramiche di Lucio Fontana. Emporium. 89:162-3 Mr 1939.

148 ZOCCHI, JUAN. Lucio Fontana. 84p. incl. 64 pl. (some col.) Buenos Aires, Poseidon, 1946. (Biblioteca argentina de arte.)

GRECO

149 ROME. GALLERIA DEL SECOLO. Emilio Greco. Prefazione di Fortunato Bellonzi. [12]p. incl. 5 il. 1948.
Catalog for exhibition held Ja 22-F 5. Reviewed in Emporium 107: 80-81 F 1948.

GUIDI

150 BREDDO, G. Virgilio Guidi. *In* Cairola, Stefano, ed. Arte italiana del nostro tempo. p.44-5 il(por.) Bergamo, Instituto italiano d'arti grafiche, 1946.

151 GATTO, ALFONSO. 12 opere di Virgilio Guidi. [8]p. plus 12 col. pl. Milano, Il Milione, 1944. (Pittori italiani contemporanei.)

152 ——— Virgilio Guidi. 18p., col.front., plus 37 il. Milan, Ulrico Hoepli, 1947 (Arte moderna italiana. 47)
Extensive bibliography, p.12-18.

153 SOLMI, SERGIO, Visita allo studio di Guidi. 2il.(col.) Lettere ed Arti 2no.7-8:36-43 Jy-Ag 1946.

GUTTUSO

154 GUTTUSO, RENATO. "Gott mit uns. . ." con una nota introduttiva di Antonello Trombadori. 10p. plus 24 pl. (some col.) Roma, La Margherita, 1945.
Drawings of German massacres in Italy. Illustrated cover.

155 ——— Lettera di Guttuso. il. Domus no.223-25:52-6 O-D 1947.

156 IL '45. Italian review of art and poetry. Nos. 1-3. Milan, Ciri Agostini, 1946.
Guttuso was on the editorial staff. A color plate is reproduced in no. 1 F 1946, and the cover of no.3, My 1946, is by the artist.

157 BARTOLINI, L. Renato Guttuso. *In* Cairola, Stefano, ed. Arte italiana del nostro tempo. p.45-6 il. (por.) Bergamo, Instituto italiana d'arti grafiche, 1946.

158 MARCHIORI, G. Momento di Guttuso. 3il. Emporium 106: 124-8 N 1947.

159 STARACE, PIPPI. Guttuso e Morandi. 1 il. Arte Contemporanea 1no.2:3 D 1946.

160 TROMBADORI, ANTONELLO. Renato Guttuso. 2il. (por.) Numero Pittura (Milan) 3no.1:7 D 15 1946.

161 WYNNE, MILTON J. A letter from Italy [on Guttuso] American Contemporary Art (New York) 1no.11:2,11 Ja 1945.

See also bibl. 10, 20, 30, 31.

LEPRI

162 Cadavres exquis, by Clerici, Fini, Lepri. il. View (New York) 6 no.1:12 F 1946.
A page of drawings.

163 HUGO GALLERY, NEW YORK. Stanislao Lepri, paintings and drawings. [4]p. il.1948.
First American exhibition held Ja 20-F 14. Includes drawings on the catalog, and biographical statement on rear cover, reviewed bibl. 165.

164 PIEYRE DE MANDIARGUES, ANDRÉ. Deux amis de Leonor Fini: Clerici et Lepri. 2il. Art et Style no.4: [65-9] Ap 1946.

165 [PRESTON, STUART] Spotlight on Lepri. 1il Art News 46 no.12:30, 49 F 1948.
Review of Hugo gallery exhibit.

MAFAI

166 MARCHIORI, GIUSEPPE. Artisti contemporanei: Mario Mafai. 12il.(por.) Emporium 92:121-8 S 1940.

167 ———Mario Mafai. Vernice (Trieste) 3no.22-23:30 Ap-My 1948.

168 PODESTÀ, ATTILIO. Mario Mafai. *In* Cairola, Stefano, ed. Arte italiana del nostra tempo. p.51-2 Bergamo, Instituto italiano d'arte grafiche, 1946.

See also bibl. 30, 31, 40, 232.

MANZÙ

169 ARGAN, GIULIO CARLO. Manzù: disegni. [10]p. plus
32 pl. (some col.) Bergamo, Instituto italiano d'arti
grafiche [1948]

170 BARTOLINI, LUIGI. Giacomo Manzù. 42p. plus 32 il.
Rovereto, Delfino, 1944.
Extensive bibliography, p.33-42.

171 JOPPOLO, BENIAMINO. Giacomo Manzù. 22p. plus 32 il.
Milan, Ulrico Hoepli, 1946. (Arte moderna italiana. 46)
Extensive bibliography, p.13-22.

172 MICHELI, MARIO DE. Manzù. [6]p. plus 24 pl. Milano,
Corrente, 1942. (Quaderni del disegno contempo-
raneo.2)

173 PACCHIONI, ANNA. Giacomo Manzù. Prefazione di
Lionello Venturi. 41p. plus 79 pl. (some col.) Milano,
Il Milione, 1948.
Extensive classified bibliography, p.30-36.

174 VIRGIL. Le Georgiche di Virgilio [Versione italiana di
Giulio Caprin, con venti acquaforti di Manzù] [126]p.
incl. 20 il. Milano, Ulrico Hoepli, 1948.
165 copies, issued loose in box.

175 VITALI, LAMBERTO. Lo scultore Giacomo Manzù. 15 il.
Emporium 87:243-54 My 1938.

MARINI

176 CARRÀ, CARLO. Marino Marini. il. Lettere ed Arti
1no.3:28-9 N 1945.

177 CARRIERI, RAFFAELE. Marino Marini, scultore. 36p.
plus 89 pl. (some col.) Milano, Il Milione, 1948.
Extensive bibliography, p.26-32.

178 CONTINI, GIANFRANCO. Vingt sculptures de Marino
Marini. 7p. plus 20 il. Lugano, Collana di Lugano,
1944.
Brief bibliography, p.11.

179 FIERENS, PAUL. Marino Marini. 8p. plus 38 pl. Paris,
Chroniques du Jour; Milan, Ulrico Hoepli, 1936. (Art
italien moderne.)
"Printed in Italy, 1936."

180 DE PISIS, FILIPPO. Marino Marini. [8]p. plus [63]pl.
Milano, Conchiglia, 1941. (Pittori e scultori italiani
contemporanei.2)
Text in Italian and German. Biographical note on plate 5,11,36,38.

181 VITALI, LAMBERTO. Marino Marini. 25p., front. (por.),
plus 33 il. Milano, Ulrico Hoepli, 1937. (Arte moderna
italiana. 29)
Extensive bibliography, p.21-25.

182 ———— Marino Marini. il. Horizon (London) 18no.105:
203-7 S 1948.

MARTINI

183 MARTINI, ARTURO. 30 disegni. [10]p. plus 30 pl.
Venezia, Piccola galleria, 1944.
"Disegni esposti alla 1ª mostra della "Piccola galleria, 8 aprile-5
maggio." Introduction by Martini.

184 ———— Una scultura. 25 leaves Venezia, Piccola
galleria, 1944.
Reproductions of a female figure seen from many angles. The only
text is a poem by Paul Valéry.

185 ———— La scultura lingua morte. Pensieri. [58]p.
Verona [Officina Bodoni] 1948.
Giovanni Mardersteig: "Al lettore," p. [53]. Originally published in
1945 with subtitle: Prima raccolta di pensieri.

186 APOLLONIO, UMBRO. Arturo Martini. 2il. Emporium
108no.613-14:69-72 Jy-Ag 1948.
Brief bibliography. Also published in bibl. 3.

187 BACCHELLI, RICCARDO. La giustizia corporativa, al-
torilievo per il Palazzo di giustizia in Milano. 15p.
plus 32 pl. Milan, Il Milione, 1937.

188 BONTEMPELLI, MASSIMO. Arturo Martini. 2.ed. 32p.,
front., plus 40 pl. Milano, Ulrico Hoepli, 1948. (Arte
moderna italiana. 23)
Extensive bibliography, p.18-32.

189 BRUNELLO, LUIGI. Arturo Martini, un sommo della
scultura. 1 il. Arte Contemporanea 2no.4-5:1 Ap-My
1947.

190 FIERENS, PAUL. Sculpteurs d'aujourd'hui. p.22-3, pl.
50-3. Paris, Chroniques du Jour; London, A. Zwemmer,
1933 (XXe siècle).
Biographical note.

191 LO DUCA, GIUSEPPE. Arturo Martini. 16p. plus 27 pl.
Milan, Ulrico Hoepli, 1933. (Arte moderna italiana. 23)

MASCHERINI

192 APOLLONIO, UMBRO. Marcello Mascherini. In Ciarola,
Stefano, ed. Arte italiana del nostro tempo. p.59-60 il.
(por.) Bergamo, Instituto italiano d'arte grafiche,
1946.

193 MARUSSI, GARIBALDO. Marcello Mascherini, premiato
alla permanente di Milano. 1il Vernice (Trieste)
3no.22-23:43 Ap-My 1948.

194 PICA, AGNOLDOMENICO. Marcello Mascherini, con uno
scritto di Giani Stuparich. 36p. plus 40 pl. Milano,
G. G. Görlich, 1945.
Extensive bibliography, p.33-6. Also issued in 15 copies with an
original drawing.

MODIGLIANI

195 APOLLONIO, UMBRO. Breve omaggio a Modigliani. 8il
(por.) Emporium 103:260-9 Je 1946.

196 BRIELLE, ROGER. Modigliani et l'inquiétude nos-
talgique. In Huyghe, René. Histoire de l'art contemporain: la peinture. p.141-4 7il (por.) Paris, Félix
Alcan, 1935.
Bibliographical and biographical notes, p.48-9.

197 CARRIERI, RAFFAELE. 12 opere di Amedeo Modigliani.
[18]p. plus 12 col. pl. Milano, Il Milione, 1947. (Pittori
italiani contemporanei.)

198 DALE, MAUD. Modigliani. 14p., col. front., plus 50 pl.
New York, A. A. Knopf, 1929.

199 DOUGLAS, CHARLES. Artist quarter. p.65-99 incl. 7 il.
London, Faber and Faber, 1941.
Modigliani in Montmartre and Montparnasse.

200 FRANCHI, RAFFAELO. Modigliani. 3.ed. 44p. plus 52 pl.
(some col.) Firenze, Arnaud, 1946.

201 PFANNSTIEL, ARTHUR. Modigliani. Préface de Louis
Latourettes. 135p. plus pl. (some col.) Paris, M.
Scheur, 1929. (L'art et la vie. 11)
Bibliography, p.131-5.

MORANDI

202 BECCARIA, ARNALDO. Giorgio Morandi. 23p., col.
front., plus 33 pl. Milano, Ulrico Hoepli, 1939. (Arte
moderna italiana. 32)
Biographical note by C. Brandi, p.17-18. Extensive bibliography,
p.19-23.

203 BRANDI, CESARE. Morandi. 43p., 2 col. pl., plus 48 il. Firenze, Le Monnier, 1942.
Bibliography, p.39-40.

204 GNUDI, CESARE. Morandi. 64p. plus 50 pl. Firenze, Editions U, 1946.

205 MARCHIORI, GIUSEPPE. Giorgio Morandi. 6 il. Domus 17no.134:66-8 F 1939.

206 PETRUCCI, CARLO ALBERTO. Le incisioni de Morandi. [8]p. 1 il [Arte grafiche Besteti] 1948.

207 PODESTÀ, ATTILIO. La lezione di Morandi. 1 il Emporium 107no.641:221-3 My 1948.

208 SCHEIWILLER, GIOVANNI. Giorgio Morandi. [10]p. plus 20 pl. (some col.) Torino, Chiantore, 194? (Artisti italiani contemporanei.)

209 VISENTINI, GINO. La pasienza di Morandi. In his Gusti esagerati. p.73-78 il. Firenze, Vallecchi, 1942.

PIRANDELLO

210 GUZZI, VIRGILIO. Fausto Pirandello. Arte Contemporanea 1no.1-1,4 O 1946.
Also published in Cairola, bibl. 7.

DE PISIS

211 DE PISIS, FILIPPO. Alcune poesie e dieci litografie a colori. [68] p. incl. il. Venezia, Il Tridente, 1945.
Edition of 310 copies, issued loose in box.

212 ——— Pittura moderna. Ferrara, 1919.
The Library lacks this title, which is "scarce and important."

213 ——— Prose e articoli. 181p. il. Milano, Il Balcone, 1947.
Essays on "arte metafisica," "Marino Marini," "Carrà e De Chirico," etc.

214 [Angiolini, Arrigo] Filippo de Pisis, pittore. 76p. incl. 24 il. Genova, Collano "Euro romano," n.d.
Bibliography, p.71-6.

215 GEORGE, WALDEMAR. F. de Pisis. [16]p. plus 24 pl. Paris, Chroniques du Jour, 1928. (Maîtres de l'art étranger.)
"Écrits par Filippo de Pisis," p. IX-[XVI]

216 MARCHIORI, G. Filippo de Pisis. 8il. Emporium 87:29-36 Ja 1938.

217 NEBBIA, UGO. Filippo de Pisis. [12]p. plus 20 col. pl. Torino, Chiantore, n.d. (Artisti italiani contemporanei.)
Also special edition of 50 copies with an original lithograph.

218 RAIMONDI, GIUSEPPE. Filippo de Pisis. [10]p., front. (por.), plus 50 pl. (some col.) Milano, Garzanti, n.d. (Monografie d'arte di "Stile.")
Bibliography by G. Scheiwiller.

219 SOLMI, SERGIO. Filippo de Pisis. 18p., col. front., plus 28 pl. Milano, Ulrico Hoepli, 1931. (Arte moderna italiana. 19)
Brief bibliography.

PIZZINATO

220 APOLLONIO, UMBRO. Armando Pizzinato. In Cairola, Stefano, ed. Arte italiano del nostro tempo. p.77-8 il. (por.) Bergamo, Instituto italiano d'arti grafiche, 1946.

ROSAI

221 ROSAI, OTTONE. Via Toscanella. 195p. il. Firenze, Vallecchi, 1930.
Drawings by Rosai, preface by Ardengo Soffici.

222 FRANCHI, RAFFAELO. Disegni di Ottone Rosai. 24p., front., plus 36 pl. Milano, Ulrico Hoepli, 1942.
Extensive bibliography, p. 15-24.

223 MASCIOTTA, MICHELANGELO. Ottone Rosai. 46p. plus 33 pl. Firenze, Parenti, 1940. (Collezione di Letteratura. 31)
Extensive bibliography, p. 41-4.

224 PARRONCHI, ALESSANDRO. Rosai. 24p. plus 39 pl. (some col.) Firenze, Arnaud, 1947. (Artisti italiani contemporanei.)
Edition of 650, of which 50 were issued with an original drawing. Bibliography, p.21.

225 VOLTA, SANDRO. Ottone Rosai. 12p., col. front., plus 29 il. Milan, Ulrico Hoepli, 1931. (Arte moderna italiana. 21)
Bibliography, p.12.

RUSSOLO

226 RUSSOLO, LUIGI. Conquista totale dell' enarmonismo mediante gl'intonarumori futuristi. Lacerba 1no.21: 242-5 N 1913.
Typical of the frequent articles by Russolo in bibl. 81.

227 BOCCIONI, UMBERTO. Pittura, scultura futuriste . . . con 51 riproduzioni . . . di Boccioni, Carrà, Russolo, Balla, Severini, Soffici. p. 451-3, 460,464 et passim,6 il. Milano, Edizioni futuriste di "Poesia," 1914.

228 DERI, MAX. Die Malerei im XIX. Jahrhundert. In zwei Bänden. p.252-8, pl. 77-84. Berlin, Paul Cassirer. 1923.
On Russolo, Boccioni and Severini.

See also bibl. 72-84.

SANTOMASO

229 PALLUCHINI, R. Bepi Santomaso. 7il. (1 col.) Emporium 95:200-5 My 1942.
Bibliography.

230 PODESTÀ, ATTILIO. Giuseppe Santomaso. In Cairola, Stefano, ed. Arte italiano del nostro tempo. p.85-6 il. (por.) Bergamo, Instituto italiano d'arte grafiche, 1946.

See also bibl. 10.

SCIALOJA

231 ROME. GALLERIA DEL SECOLO. Ciarrocchi, Sadun, Scialoja, Stradone [4]p. plus il. Rome, 1947.
Exhibition held March, including 6 works by Toti Scialoja. Preface by Cesare Brandi.

SCIPIONE

232 SCIPIONE. Carte segrete. Raccolte a cura di Enrico Falqui. 121p. Firenze, Vallecchi, 1943.
Poems and essays, including letters to Mario Mafai and others. Bibliographic notes, p.117.

233 Vita e leggenda di Scipione. 1il. Le Tre Arti 2no.3:3 Mr-Ap 1946.
Extract from "Carte segrete" and introduction by Enrico Falqui.

234 APOLLONIO, UMBRO. Scipione. [22]p. plus 11 pl. Venezia, Cavallino, 1945.

235 MALTESE, CORRADO. Scipione. 6il Emporium 108no. 613-4:73-8 Jy-Ag 1948.
Also published in bibl. 3.

236 ——— Presentazione di alcuni inediti di Scipione. il. Emporium 108no.647:226-32. N 1948.

237 MARCHIORI, GIUSEPPE. Disegni di Scipione. 14p. plus 30 pl. Bergamo, Instituto italiano d'arti grafiche, 1944. (Disegnatori ed. incisatori italiani.8)
Bibliography, p.11.

238 SANTANGELO, ANTONIO. Scipione. [4]p. plus 6 pl. (5 col.) [Milano?, Edizioni di Corrente, 1941]
Issued under the supervision of Duilio Morosini for the exhibition at the Pinacoteca, Brera in March. Same text included in regular exhibition catalog: "Scipione, mostra postume a cura del Centro di Azione per le Arti regia pinacoteca di Brera." Issued as insert to Corrente folder, advertised as "Cinque tricromie," which contains, in library copy, 5 color plates and an additional illustration.

239 SINISGALLI, LEONARDO. Disegni di Scipione. [4]p. plus 12 pl. Venezia, Cavallino, 1942.
Preface titled: I 12 mesi di Scipione.

240 VISENTINI, GINO. L'inferno di Scipione. In his Gusti esagerati. p.67-72 il Firenze, Vallecchi, 1942.

SEMEGHINI

240aMARCHIORI, GIUSEPPE. Pio Semeghini. p.89-90 (por.) In Cairola, Stefano, ed. Arte italiana. See bibl. 7.

SEVERINI

241 SEVERINI, GINO. Tutta la vita di un pittore. Volume primo: Roma-Parigi. 274p. plus pl. Cernusco sul Naviglio, Garzanti, 1946.

242 BILLIET—CAPUTO GALLERY, PARIS. Severini, oeuvres anciennes et récentes. [16]p. 4 il. Paris, 1947.
Exhibit held My 21-Je 21. Statement by Pierre Courthion. Bibliography, p.[11-13]

243 BULLETIN DE L'EFFORT MODERNE. Directeur: Léonce Rosenberg. Paris, 1924-27.
Severini is frequently reproduced in, and made contributions to the following issues: no.7 Jy 1924, no.8 O 1924, no.14 Ap 1925, no.18 O 1925, no.19 N 1925, no.20 D 1925, no.28 O 1926, no.30 D 1926, no.31 Ja 1927, no.32 F 1927, no.33 Mr 1927, no.35 My 1927, no.36-37 Je 1927.

244 COURTHION, PIERRE. Gino Severini. 17p., col. front., plus 29 pl. Milano, Ulrico Hoepli, 1930. (Arte moderna italiana. 17)
Bibliography, p.15-17.

245 MARITAIN, JACQUES. Severini. 63p. incl. 47 pl. Paris, Gallimard, 1930. (Peintres nouveaux. 40)
Text, p.2-16. Essay on "Gino Severini" also published in his: Art and poetry. p.30-8 New York, Philosophical library, 1943.

246 WALL, BERNARD. Gino Severini. In Severini, Gino. The artist in society. p. vi-viii London, Harvill press, 1946. (Changing world series.1)
Essays translated by B. Wall.

SIRONI

247 ANCESCHI, LUCIANO. Mario Sironi. [18]p., 3 il. (2 col.) plus 79 pl. Milano, Conchiglia, 1944. (Pittori e scultori italiani contemporanei.V)
Bibliography, p.[11-12]

248 BONTEMPELLI, MASSIMO. 12 tempere di Mario Sironi . . . con dichiarazione dell' artista. [10]p. plus 12 col. pl. Milano, Il Milione, n.d. (Pittori italiani contemporanei.)

249 BROGLIO, MARIO. Mostra Sironi. Valori Plastici 1no. 6-10: 29-30 Je-O 1919.

250 SARTORIS, ALBERTO. Mario Sironi. 35p., col. front., plus 37 il. Milano, Ulrico Hoepli, 1946. (Arte moderna italiana. 18)
Extensive bibliography, p.23-35.

251 SCHEIWILLER, GIOVANNI. Mario Sironi. [18]p., col. front. plus 28 pl. Milan, Ulrico Hoepli, 1930. (Arte moderna italiana. 18)

SOFFICI

252 SOFFICI, ARDENGO. Rete mediterranea. 382p. il. Firenze, Vallecchi, 1920.
Partial contents: "Pittura metafisica," p.77-8. Apologia del futurismo, p.197-207. Tre giovani artisti italiani [Rosai, Galante, Garbari] p.372-4.

253 —— Ricordi di vita artistica e letteraria. 2.ed. 426p. Firenze, Vallecchi, 1942.

254 MARCHIORI, G. Ardengo Soffici, 13 il.(por.) Emporium 85:174-86 Ap 1937.
Bibliography.

255 PAPINI, GIOVANNI. 12 opere di Ardengo Soffici. [10]p. plus 12 col. pl. Milano, Il Milione, 1945. (Pittori italiani contemporanei.)

TOSI

256 ARGAN, GIULIO CARLO. Tosi. 39p., 2 col.pl., plus 48 il. Firenze, Le Monnier, 1942. (Biblioteca di storia dell' arte.)
Bibliography, p.35-6.

257 GEORGE, WALDEMAR. A. Tosi, peintre classique et peintre rustique. 11p. plus 36 pl. Paris, Chroniques du Jour; Milan, Hoepli, 1933.
Brief bibliography.

258 NEBBIA, UGO. Un inverno a Rovetta. [10]p. plus 12 col. pl. Milano, Il Milione, 1944. (Pittori italiani contemporanei.)

259 SCHEIWILLER, GIOVANNI. Arturo Tosi. [18]p., front. (por.), plus 50 pl. (some col.) Milano, Garzanti 1942. (Monografie d'arte di "Stile.")
Extensive bibliography.

VESPIGNANI

259aFLEMING, JOHN. Renzo Vespignani. In Orpheus, Vol:1. 4 il.(por.) p.120-2 London, John Lehmann, 1948.

VIANI

260 Sculture di Alberto Viani. 29p. plus 10 pl. Milano, Spiga, 1946.
"Testimonianze di Anceschi, Apollonio, Bettini, Birolli, Emanuelli, Guidi, Marchiori, Martini, Pallucchini, Valsecchi."

261 BIROLLI, RENATO. Alberto Viani. In Cairola, Stefano, ed. Arte italiano del nostro tempo. p.101-2 il.(por.) Bergamo, Instituto italiano d'arte grafiche, 1946.

VIVIANI

262 LIBERO, LIBERO DE. Sei incisioni di Giuseppe Viviani. [6]p.plus 6 pl. Milano, "all 'Insegna del Pesce d'Oro," 1947.
With foreword by the artist, p.[2]

This book has been printed in June, 1949, for the Trustees of the Museum of Modern Art, New York, by the Plantin Press, New York. The color plates were printed by the John B. Watkins Company, New York. Cover and jacket design by George Giusti.